THE POLITICS
OF
INTERNATIONAL STANDARDS

France and the Color TV War

COMMUNICATION AND
INFORMATION SCIENCE

A series of monographs,
treatises, and texts

Edited by
MELVIN J. VOIGT

University of California, San Diego

RHONDA J. CRANE ● The Politics of International Standards: France and the
Color TV War
VINCENT MOSCO ● Broadcasting in the United States: Innovative Challenge
and Organizational Control
KAARLE NORDENSTRENG and HERBERT I. SCHILLER ● National
Sovereignty and International Communication: A Reader

In Preparation

JOHN J. GEYER ● Reading as Information Processing
MICHEL GUITE ● Telecommunications Policy: The Canadian Model
JOHN S. LAWRENCE and BERNARD M. TIMBERG ● Copyright Law, Fair Use
and the New Media
ROBERT G. MEADOW ● Politics as Communication
ITHIEL DE SOLA POOL ● Retrospective Technology Assessment of the
Telephone
CLAIRE K. SCHULTZ ● Computer History and Information Access

THE POLITICS
OF
INTERNATIONAL STANDARDS

France and the Color TV War

RHONDA J. CRANE

ABLEX Publishing Corporation
Norwood, New Jersey 07648

Printed in the United States of America.

Library of Congress Cataloging in Publication Data

Crane, Rhonda J.
    The politics of international standards.

    (Communication and information science)
    Bibliography: p.
    Includes indexes.
    1. Television industry—France.   2. Color
television—Receivers and reception—Standards.
3. Standardization—Case studies.   4. Telecommunication—International cooperation—Case
studies.   I. Title.   II. Series.
HD9999.T373F82   384.55'0944   79-4231
ISBN   0-89391-019-8

ABLEX Publishing Corporation
355 Chestnut Street
Norwood, New Jersey 07648

for my mother
Paula Crane
in memory of my father
Professor Bertram Roswell Crane

Contents

3

The Development of French Policy
to Create a Color Television Industry 37

4

The Development
of an Export Market
for SECAM 53

5

SECAM: French Ambitions
and International Outcome 71

6

Foreword

The negotiation and enactment of technical standards is a form of political behavior that is largely unanalyzed in the social science literature. Social scientists are interested in conflict resolution, coalition formation, lawmaking, market segmentation, and social change. The setting of technical standards involves and illuminates all of those topics, yet social scientists have said little about it.

A variety of social systems (including communication systems) can function only when parties with conflicting interests agree on what technical characteristics to build into products that are used.

The example about which Rhonda Crane writes, the adoption of color television standards in France, is a case in point; it is an instance of international bargaining and attempted international legislation. What was at issue was whether standards adopted in France would be compatible with those used in the television systems of other countries. Just as domestic standard-setting has all the classic problems of legislative struggle, so international standard-setting incorporates all the dilemmas of international relations. Agreement on standards—or refusal to adopt common standards—is one of the most important nontariff devices to facilitate international trade, or to restrict it, to strengthen cooperative alliance, or to prevent it.

Rhonda Crane is opening up this largely unstudied terrain. She tells a fascinating story of Gaullist nationalist politics. A unique set of French standards was used as a device for creating a French industry protected from outside competition and for creating a sphere of international French influence in the cultural arena. It was a gambit that worked, though at the expense of broader international intercourse and cooperation, on the desirability of which virtually everyone else was agreed. It is thus the story of a successful political ploy buried in a technological argument.

The range of areas in which politics is played in international organizations under the guise of technical issues is growing. Among such debates, one might mention the law of the sea, spectrum allocation, and energy development. In all these debates, politicians are often unsure what is at stake. Engineers are apt to think the solution should be purely technical. In the end, unexpected outcomes may be produced by negotiators who are clever enough to understand what political gains may be achieved by some technical detail.

There is at least one other reason why we should understand the standard-setting process better. No doubt, standards must be set if there is to be cooperative development of any new device, but at the same time the premature setting of standards prevents future and, perhaps superior innovations. The history of video tape recorders in recent years is a case in point. People involved in the development of video communication have fumed at the incompatibility between the various machines made by different manufacturers. There has been a repeated call for standards. But in the dynamic field, would standards have helped or would they have prevented the development of the newer improved methods now coming on the market? I do not know. We need much more study of the effects of standard-setting.

Such questions are addressed in this book. It opens up a major subject. We may hope that other students will follow Dr. Crane and look at other cases, as Dr. Crane has looked at the case of French color TV.

ITHIEL DE SOLA POOL
Massachusetts Institute of Technology

Preface

This project has absorbed almost three years of my life, two of them full-time. It was conceived initially as a term paper, but the unanswered questions quickly led me to consider its merit as a disertation topic, and later as a book. No prior work existed which could provide an orientation or interpretation of the facts. This meant that research was required both in France and in the United States. Furthermore, this was an area for political scientists where virtually no field literature was available. Perhaps its fascination for me stemmed from its great challenge. In 1975 I spent about three months in France, Switzerland, Belgium, and Germany, tracking down the main authorities on the French participation in color television development. I had three fears when I first arrived in Paris: Would the responsible French officials see me? Would they talk honestly with me? And, if I understood them, would I have the substance for an interesting thesis? I was rewarded by warmth, generosity, cooperation, and an intriguing story. It is with mingled joy and deep regret that I concluded it.

ACKNOWLEDGMENTS

I have thoroughly enjoyed working on this book. Several people have contributed at various stages to its development, most of all Professor Ithiel de Sola Pool of M.I.T. Professor Pool's influence has guided my thinking and approach since it first appeared on his desk in embryonic form as a term paper some years ago. His encouragement has been the source of my strength in carrying it through to its present form. I have profound respect and admiration for his judgment, and am deeply honored and grateful that he wrote the Foreword and that I have had the superb experience of working with him. Professor Suzanne Berger of M.I.T. enthusiastically participated in all phases of this work. Professor Berger advised me in the structuring of this project from the research design to the organization of the chapters. Her assistance and advice were invaluable. Professor Harvey Sapolsky of M.I.T. was responsible for suggesting the topic initially and also provided numerous ideas and improvements to its formulation. Professor Eugene Skolnikoff of M.I.T. also made substantial contributions to this work. His comments, advice, criticisms, and ideas have formed the basis for many new perceptions developed while writing the chapters. I am deeply indebted to all of these persons for their help, time, trouble, and care.

In addition, there are more than one hundred people in France without whom this book could never have been written. These people permitted me to interview them, utilize their valuable time, and sometimes they responded to requests for information that was difficult for them to retrieve. Much of the material is based on interviews with present and former French officials, politicians, former advisers to President de Gaulle, engineers, journalists, broadcasting experts, electronics industry executives, members of the O.R.T.F., and other industrial and governmental advisers. Additional material was obtained at the International Exhibition of Electronic Components held at Porte de Versailles, Paris, in 1975, and from interviews with members of the French and other European delegations to the 1965 Vienna conference of the C.C.I.R. I am grateful to all of these persons for their help and thank them collectively, since they were promised anonymity. Information was also obtained from many technical experts in the United States.

Other people whose aid has also benefited this work are: Donna Roizen and Joseph Roizen, president of TELEGEN Corporation (for permission to use the Television World map); the Export Bureau of the Department of Commerce (for release of the ACEP—VTR documents); Monsieur Dubail, INTERSECAM (for permission to use various documents in the research); the Center for International Studies and Sloan School Program for International Business (for a dissertation research award); and Harold Strudler esq. and Theodore Thau esq. (for enormous support and encouragement). The final stages of this project probably would have been delayed many years if not for the help of Dr. Martin Wilk, assistant vice president of Corporate Planning at AT&T. Dr. Wilk afforded me the opportunity to finish it and graciously provided the facilities and atmosphere conducive to its completion. My colleagues, Dr. Blaine Davis and Dr. Tom O'Brien, managers of Corporate Planning, AT&T, have also been highly supportive and most understanding during the last months of the project. Mrs. Manuela Otero has provided the skillful final touches with her expert typing, patient care, and long hours of cheerful assistance. Thank you, everyone.

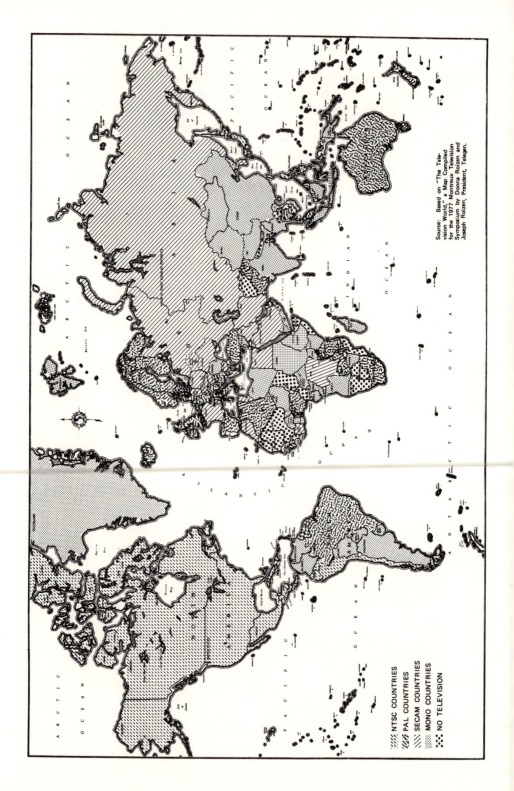

Source: Based on "The Television World," a Map Compiled
for the 1977 Montreux Television
Symposium by Donna Roizen and
Joseph Roizen, President, Telegen.

NTSC COUNTRIES
PAL COUNTRIES
SECAM COUNTRIES
MONO COUNTRIES
NO TELEVISION

The Color Television World*

NTSC Countries	PAL Countries	SECAM Countries	MONO Countries	No Television
Antigua, West Indies	Algeria	Afars & Issac	Albania	Afghanistan
Bahamas	Australia	Arab Republic of Egypt	Angola	Botswana
Barbados	Austria	Bulgaria	Argentina	Burma
British Virgin Islands	Bahrain	Czechoslovakia	Bolivia	Cambodia
Canada	Bangladesh	France	Central African Republic	Cameroon
Chile	Belgium	East Germany	People's Republic of China	Chad
Costa Rica	Brazil (PAL M)	Greece	Colombia	Guyana
Cuba	Brunei	Haiti	Comoro Islands	Laos
Dominican Republic	Denmark	Hungary	Cyprus	Malawi
Ecuador	Federal Republic of Germany	Iran	Equatorial Guinea	Mali
El Salvador	Finland	Ivory Coast	Ethiopia	Mauritania
Guatemala	Hong Kong	Iraq	French Guiana	Mozambique
Japan	Iceland	Lebanon	French Polynesia	Nepal
Mexico	Ireland	Luxembourg	Gabon	Somalia
Netherlands Antilles, West Indies	Italy	Mauritius	Ghana	South West Africa
Nicaragua	Jordan	Monaco	Gibraltar	Spanish Sahara
Panama	Kuwait	Morocco	Guadeloupe	Sri Lanka
Peru	Malaysia	Poland	Honduras	
Philippines	Netherlands	Reunion	India	
St. Kitts, West Indies	New Zealand	Saudi Arabia	Indonesia	
Samoa (U.S.)	Nigeria	Tunisia	Israel	
Surinam	Norway	USSR	Jamaica	
Taiwan (Province of)	Oman	Zaire	Kenya	
Trinidad, West Indies	Pakistan		Khmer Republic	
Trust Territory of Pacific	Qatar		Liberia	
United States	Singapore		Libyan Arab Republic	
	South Africa		Malta	
	Spain		Malagasy Republic	
	Sweden		Martinique	
	Switzerland		New Calendonia	
	Tanzania		Niger	
	Thailand		Paraguay	
	Turkey		People's Democratic Republic of Korea	
	United Arab Emirates		People's Democratic Republic of Yemen	
	United Kingdom		Portugal	
	Yugoslavia		Republic of the Congo	
	Zambia		Republic of Vietnam	
			Rhodesia	
			Romania	
			Senegal	
			Sierra Leone	
			St. Pierre & Miquelon	
			Sudan	
			Syria	
			Uganda	
			Upper Volta	
			Uruguay	
			Venezuela	
			Yemen Arab Republic	

*Source: Based on "The Television World", a map compiled for the 1977 Montreux Television Symposium by Donna Roizen and Joseph Roizen, President, TELEGEN.

THE POLITICS
OF
INTERNATIONAL STANDARDS

France and the Color TV War

1

Communication Standards and the Politics of Protectionism

INTRODUCTION

Communication between nations forms the foundation upon which international understanding is built. Countries need the ability to communicate with one another, but the mere possession of technical systems does not ensure that transmission and reception is possible between them. Compatible standards for the technical systems are necessary before communication can take place.

Competing national interests frequently intervene in efforts to establish compatible standards for communication systems and thus make international agreement unfeasible. While incompatibility can be surmounted in some instances by technological developments, circumstances created by an inability to communicate may have severe consequences.

Visualize what could happen if an airplane equipped with microwave landing gear were forced to make an emergency landing at a foreign airport with an incompatible system, and the pilot could not communicate with the control tower (Air traffic control, 1965; Robertson, 1976; Technology: A bitter dispute, 1975). Imagine the economic repercussions if conditions required the urgent computer transmission of bulk financial data to banks in different countries, and incompatible standards prevented the terminals from receiving the information. Or, on a different level, consider the inconvenience, expense, and delays for broadcasters when the exchange of programs between nations operating on different standards necessitates elaborate conversion procedures (Franklin, 1966; Weller, 1966).

1

If these are examples of problems which can arise whenever standards for technical systems are incompatible, what prevents nations from adopting compatible standards at the outset?

A basic dilemma underlies the development of international telecommunications, a dilemma nations encounter each time they are forced to choose between standards for different technical systems of communication. The focal point of the dilemma for each nation is the determination of the relative advantages or disadvantages of standards compatibility: Do the advantages of compatibility and the ability to communicate with other nations outweigh the advantages of incompatibility, the ability to protect domestic industries, or control broadcasts or information transmitted across national airwaves?

In the following chapters, some of the facets of this dilemma are explored in an analysis of the failure to establish internationally compatible technical standards for color television systems. Through a case study of France, the problems involved in the international selection of a European standard for color television systems are examined.

Three different color television systems (developed by the United States, France, and West Germany) were in competition to become the European standard. All three color television systems were incompatible with one another; broadcasts transmitted on one system could not be received on television sets manufactured for a different system. Therefore, there was international interest in the adoption of a single color television standard for all of Europe. The competition between the systems to become the European standard was politically intense; the nation whose system was selected as the European standard would gain large economic revenues and political prestige.

In order to fulfill their ambitions to develop a color television industry and create an export market for the products, the French sought to make their system the European standard. The French were interested in adopting compatible color television standards with the rest of Europe, on condition that the French system would be chosen as the European standard so that France could recoup financial investments from patent and license royalties. If another system were chosen as the European standard, the French could ensure the development of their color television industry with different standards, by creating a different market for the products in Communist, Third World, and less developed countries. The difference in technical standards between the three systems also could be employed as a nontariff barrier to protect the French color television industry during its developmental stages.

Three major themes are investigated.

First, what are the problems that are generated by having differences in national technical standards in communications? Are differences in technical standards effective tools to create an industry?

Second, when and how may a state successfully intervene to support the development of an industry in the private sector? What are some of the problems a government encounters in the promotion of an industry?

Finally, how do political and economic interests influence the course of decision-making in international organizations? What are some of the difficulties confronted by international organizations in attempting to reach international agreements on technological issues?

A discussion of the role of technology in politics is important to understanding the three themes to be explored.

TECHNOLOGICAL POLITICS

Technology is conventionally regarded as a force in world politics, affecting international relations through its diffusion, potential applications, and regulation. Technological developments occurring in one nation may have a profound impact on other nations on the other side of the globe (e.g., Holland, 1968, p. 37; Humphrey, 1968, pp. 68-69; Westfall, 1966, pp. 64-69; Wingert, 1966, pp. 67-69). This interactive effect is likely not only to continue but to expand. With increasing frequency, new technologies are emerging which are global in nature and require the participation or cooperation of many countries, if the full scope of their benefits is to be realized (Skolnikoff, 1967, pp. 302-316; Wallenstein, 1974, pp. 33-38).

In the field of communications, satellites offer the best illustration of this growing trend, with their potential for global use in meteorology, forestry, agriculture, geography, resource mapping, communications, direct broadcasting, data gathering and distribution, navigation and traffice control (Skolnikoff, 1972, pp. 56-62).

The growing applications and continuing advances of technologies such as these are generating important new demands and creating new constraints on the independence of national action. There has been a steady decrease in a nation's freedom of action to apply science and technology as it so chooses, even within its own borders (Skolnikoff, 1967, p. 303).

These pressures are evident in the increasing number of international conflicts over the possession and deployment of technological developments. For many reasons, economic, political, and military, among others, perhaps all technologies have been affected to some degree. Nations have become increasingly aware and more vocal about the technological business of their neighbors. The technological developments of one nation are objects of intense scrutiny by others. When one nation develops an important technology, rivalry develops among other nations to duplicate or improve it.

Increased international concern over technological developments has led to changes in the assessment of a nation's power. Since World War II, scientific and technological developments have sharply altered established relationships among nations and overturned traditional measures of power and influence (Skolnikoff, 1967, p. 3). A nation no longer measures its strength in military or economic terms alone, but on its technological capacity as well.

One effect of this trend has been an attempt by certain nations to impress other nations with a forceful display of technologies and, in particular, spectacular technologies. The demonstration of one nation's technological abilities requires another nation to surpass these feats, if technological pride and parity are to be maintained. For example, when the Soviet Union launched satellites and put a man into space, the United States retained its technological position by also launching satellites and then placing men on the moon. The Soviets countered by sustaining the duration of men in space, the Americans upheld their position by developing the space shuttle, and so on.

Nations vie with one another to obtain the latest technological developments. Technological strategies vary from heavy governmental support across a broad range of development, to specialization in particular areas of development, to importing another nation's advances, to some combination of the three (Gilpin, 1970). Regardless of the strategy employed to garner technological developments, the underlying assumption remains the same: namely, the greater the show of technological force, the more influence a nation may exert in the international arena. In effect, technological politics have become one of the new battlegrounds for international influence.

In many European countries, the role of technology in the political process was perceived by governments as a means of advancing and retaining political and economic power (Gilpin, 1968). This was one reason why European states intervened to support the development of industries in the private sector. The ramifications of when and how this occurred is one theme explored in this study. A motivating factor was the pereceived threat by European countries of an economic invasion from the United States. They feared the potential colonization of their economy and the concommitant loss of their political independence. Each technological advance identified as American was viewed somewhat suspiciously by European nations which sensed a further setback for themselves in a "technology gap" (Servan-Schreiber, 1967; see also Salomon, 1971; Spencer, 1970).

The French, perhaps more than other Europeans, were particularly sensitive to American technological power. At the international level, France sought to forge a "system of scientific-technological alliances that could effectively balance American power." The goal in France was "to make science an instrument of French economic, military and political objectives" (Gilpin, 1967, p. 7). Industrial development and protectionism were essential elements of this goal.

Although problems might be generated through protectionism (for example, difficulties arising from differences in communication standards with color television systems), the standards could be employed as effective tools to create an industry. While the growth of technological interdependence has led to increasing national and international pressures for countries to cooperate in selecting technologies with compatible technical standards, from the French perspective the advantages of installing incompatible standards were greater. This was particularly the case when the incompatibility could assist in the development of French technological power.

There are many difficulties that have to be overcome in the establishment of internationally compatible technical standards.

THE POLITICS OF SETTING INTERNATIONAL STANDARDS IN COMMUNICATIONS

One problem in setting standards is the question of where the responsibility lies within a country for determining the standards to be selected. This is a problem of national as well as international regulation. There are a variety of national institutional modes of authority for determining standards within a nation, but the increasing technological interdependence of countries has not been matched by the development of international mechanisms with the power to resolve conflicts among them. Consequently, difficulties persist in agreeing upon internationally compatible standards.

The significance of national standards in a commercial industry is well illustrated by the case of color television systems. Once television standards have been adopted by a nation, it is expensive to change them. For any such change, a nation must determine whether it is politically and economically advisable to scrap all television sets in use, regardless of age, condition, price, etc., because they are incompatible with the proposed new standards. Another consideration is the cost of changing all the professional electronic equipment necessary to transmit on a new system. Can this be accomplished within a political process with many vested interests? Financial pressures often lock nations into the standards they have chosen so that if standards are incompatible initially, they are likely to remain that way.

Trade in the products affected by the differences in standards may be limited to markets which use the same standards. Markets are fragmented by the existence of incompatible standards (Allen, 1966; Standards: Barriers or aids, 1970). This may lessen the economics of scale possible in mass production; it may also lessen the number of potential suppliers for each standard. This is important when the size of the market for a particular technology is taken into account. For example, according to forecasts of the electronics industry, by the 1980s sales of color television sets are expected to be worth $12 billion annually (Electronic Industries Assn., 1972). In addition, there is the multibillion dollar business in electronics equipment and components associated with the systems. This market could be better exploited by more nations if compatible technical standards existed (Standardization and the development of trade, 1964). Then production costs could be lowered and export opportunities broadened.

Communications problems are created by a lack of compatibility between systems. For example, program exchanges between countries operating on different color television systems become very difficult; elaborate conversion techniques must be employed. This lowers the technical quality of the broadcast, raises program costs, and unnecessarily complicates the exchange. Television reception problems are further exacerbated in some nations possessing linguistic and cultural diversity.

For example, in Belgium or Switzerland, the choice between the French and German standards in color television had to be weighed against the political consequences of satisfying only part of the population (Business international: Colour TV—Belgian cockpit, 1966, pp. 289-90). Ultimately, the choice would play a role in determining whether broadcasts would be received from France or from Germany. When standards are incompatible between neighboring countries, regions in border areas are also affected. Although multistandard sets capable of receiving broadcasts from different standards exist, they are very expensive. Not all viewers affected by incompatible standards are able to afford these sets.

Yet, it is difficult to establish compatible standards. As previously mentioned, there is the political problem of regulation in standard-setting at both the national and international levels. At the national level, the degree of authority within an agency to decide on a particular standard may vary from country to country. The issues of concern for that agency may not always be similar to other domestic political and economic interests. Technical compatibility may be less important to the overall national welfare than the possibility of controlling information transmitted across the country or promoting industrial development. The recommendations of a domestic agency advocating the adoption of compatible standards may be sacrificed in favor of other objectives.

Political and economic interests may negatively influence the outcome of attempts to establish compatible standards when the standards in question are linked to domestically owned patent and license rights. In such situations, the economic rewards from patent and license rights to a technology may be so great that a country simply cannot afford to sacrifice the economic interests of domestic industry in favor of the technical convenience of sharing another nation's standard. Moreover, differences in standards may provide a country with leverage to protect its industry from market invasion from the industry of another country. It is difficult for an industry to recoup the losses from the development of a technology without the royalties from patent and licensing rights, unless it is successful in capturing markets in other countries. Such economic losses may stymie future technological innovation in industry. The difference in standards might be part of that nation's objective in protecting the technology. This would mean no agreement (other than an agreement to adopt its standards) would be possible on compatible standards without a fundamental change in that nation's policies.

It is not a question of adopting an apolitical standard, but a standard that is identified with another country, a standard which symbolizes that nation's power and progress through technology. For one country to be dependent upon another for its technology may be economically as well as psychologically untenable. What happens to the dependent one, if relations beteween the two become hostile? Are supplies cut? Does the technology involved cease to function because replacement parts are not forthcoming? These factors, described in Chapter 3, influenced decisions by the French government not to be dependent upon American technology during the 1960s.

When a country equates the development and adoption of its standard with its prestige, it may not be politically feasible later to renounce that standard and adopt another one. Consequently, negotiations may break down and a deadlock occur. This is what happened with the color television systems negotiations in Vienna in 1965 during the meeting of the C.C.I.R. (International Radio Consultative Committee of the I.T.U., International Telecommunications Union) to decide which of the three (German, French, or American) color television systems to adopt as the standard for western Europe.

National political objectives in international relations may also play a role in determining the likelihood of establishing compatible standards. In the international arena, a nation's preference for adopting compatible standards may be perceived as having other important implications. When one nation votes in favor of another nation's standards, the vote may also be interpreted as a signal against a third nation. Many of the votes cast by the countries represented at the 1965 C.C.I.R. conference in Vienna were intended as political signals.

In sum, each nation approaches the issue of compatible standards with a parochial point of view. The determination of whether it is necessary as well as desirable to adopt standards compatible with other nations will be based upon an evaluation of several factors involving the national interest. These include national political strategy, national technical needs, public opinion, estimates of the value of the services, economic status, balance of payments, the costs of not agreeing, history, and experience. Once standards have been adopted, it is virtually impossible to change them.

On the organizational level, the international mechanisms for debate, negotiations, and agreement on standards—especially in communications—lack the authority to impose a solution. One of the principal difficulties in the international standardization of communication technologies arises from the existence of multiple international organizations. Each organization has an interest in a particular aspect of the standardization process. Lack of coordination and poor exchange of information among them sometimes lead to project duplication or support of conflicting standards (U.S. participation in I.E. C., 1966, p. 239).

The formation of regional blocs and regional standardization organizations contributes to this problem. When standards are adopted in regional organizations prior to being considered or recommended by world standardizing bodies, major obstacles to international cooperation are created. Positions become hardened, interests become vested, and change becomes unlikely (U.S. participation in I.E.C., 1966, p. 239). This is particularly true when standards are formulated to erect barriers to importing the goods of nonparticipating nations.

Another set of problems in the international standardization of communication technologies at the organizational level is generated by the nature of international organizations. International organizations are dependent upon their various members for financial support and technical input (La Que, 1969, p. 145). This is especially troublesome when the international organizations have a voluntary rather than government-affiliated status. In the former instance, success in adopting compatible standards is, to a greater extent, contingent upon the ability of members to submerge insular outlooks and press for cooperation, provided that the selection of compatible standards does not conflict with their national interests.

Agreement on compatible standards in international organizations is also hampered by differences in language (Ainsworth, 1964, p. 365). The need for interpretation facilities raises costs and tends to make the scheduling of frequent meetings improbable. Elaborate procedures within these international organizations are often devised to avoid areas of political sensitivity and bias. For example, committees are formed with as broad a geographical and political representation as possible. In the case of color television systems, each of the eleven subcommittees assigned to test the systems included representatives of different nations in order to prevent the interest of one country from dominating the others. Frequently, members are allowed to state publicly their reservations about particular decisions; issues where an impasse has been reached or where agreement seems unlikely may be dropped. Often, a Byzantine quality exists regarding the nature of negotiating most international compromises (Remley, 1966, p. 44).

Although such efforts are made to maintain as impartial and apolitical an atmosphere as possible within international organizations in the communications field, it is not always possible to do so. For example, in the 1965 Plenipotentiary Conference of the International Telecommunications Union at Montreux, Switzerland, a resolution to expel South Africa from the meeting was introduced by some African nations and upheld by the majority of the participants (New nations show muscle, 1965, p. 71). It is not inconceivable that similar actions might be enforced in the future with regard to Israel, Taiwan, etc. The enormous power accumulated by the Arab nations from oil wealth makes them formidable contenders should they desire to wield their influence in these international organizations.

Another group of problems which thwart negotiations at the organizational level arises from circumstances external to the nature of the international organization. These are problems of a logistical nature, including restrictions on the number of active participants (large working parties of 100 members in some organizations are not unusual, although they tend to make slow progress); time allotted for drawing up recommendations and clearing disputes (many meetings convene for at least five weeks); and the financing of participants. In the case of the United States, members or their companies must often pay their own way. Influencing decisions regarding standards in international organizations may be very expensive. Members also must take leaves of absence from their companies. Since top technical personnel are frequently involved, this may result in losses to the company (Jones, 1973, p. 207; see also Wallenstein, 1972, p. 370).

There are several factors which influence the success of a technical decision to set compatible standards for a communications technology. The case of color television systems illustrates the difficulties a government faces in the attempt to utilize differences in standards to create an industry. In the following chapters, the political and economic pressures within France which made a decision to adopt another nation's technology, another nation's standard untenable, will be explored. They are typical of the pressures other nations encounter in the dilemma of choosing internationally compatible standards. This book examines how political and economic interests influence the course of decision-making in international organizations, often conflicting with each other and with the goals of establishing compatible technical standards.

2

Historical and Technical Factors Affecting Color Television Operations

The final failure of the C.C.I.R.'s work in this field is now well known; it was not possible to recommend one unique system for 625-line colour television. All that could be achieved was a Report listing the characteristics of the "different colour television systems in use or taken into consideration at the time of the XIth Plenary Assembly of the C.C.I.R., Oslo 1966." (Hansen, 1966, p. 138)

INTRODUCTION

Since World War II, work had been proceeding on color television in Europe. When it became clear that several countries were on the verge of starting regular color television services, high priority was attached to finding uniform color television standards in international broadcasting organizations responsible for broadcast exchanges. Representatives to these organizations felt that "it was bad enough to have incompatible black-and-white systems—in the United Kingdom, France, western and eastern Europe—but much worse to permit two color television systems" (Paulu, 1970, p. 236).

Incompatible color television systems would impose numerous disadvantages on program exchanges among countries possessing different systems: recordings on one standard would not operate on another; elaborate conversion techniques would be necessitated; program costs would be raised; the exchange of programs would be complicated, and the technical quality lowered. The situation could create problems for countries with cultural and linguistic diversity—Belgium, Switzerland, Northern Italy, border regions in France and Germany, etc. (Paulu, 1970, p. 34; see also Dizard, 1966). Moreover, different broadcasting methods would disrupt Eurovision's exchange of programs. Eleven years of strenuous international efforts in testing and debating the technical merits of various color television systems failed to lead to a single standard for all of Europe. Charges and countercharges ended in a deadlock. The result was that Europe, already divided by incompatible monochrome (black-and-white) systems, was fragmented further by color television.

This chapter is divided into three sections concerning the background of historical and technical factors affecting color television operations: the system, the lines standards, and broadcasting. It illustrates the interplay of technical, political, and economic factors when international agreement is sought in the standardization of communications technologies.

COLOR TELEVISION: THE SYSTEMS

The definition of what is included in a television system is:

A chain of equipment needed to electronically "photograph" an object (or scene), encode the image and transmit the representative signal voltages whether by cable (closed circuit) or electro-magnetic waves (transmitter), decode the signal voltages and display the original image on a receiver all in snychronization with an associated audio channel. The system may include any or all accessory apparatus necessary for controlling or enhancing the transmitted image. (Roman, 1967, p. 2)

The television receiving set in a viewer's home is only one link in all the machinery necessary to broadcast television programs. Cameras, recorders, transmitters, and other equipment compose what is known as the television system. Television systems vary, not only in the type of equipment used, but also in the way the equipment is geared to broadcast.

A Comparison of NTSC, PAL, and SECAM

Historical roots. The first system that could actually transmit pictures in color was pioneered by John L. Baird in Great Britain in 1928. Approximately 12 color television systems were created during the period 1928 to 1942 in Europe, The United States, and the Soviet Union (Roman, 1967, p. 13).

In the United States, the NTSC (National Television System Committee) System, originally developed by RCA, was formally adopted in 1954, together with the single-lines standard of 525 lines for both monochrome and color television. The selection of this system in the United States had been preceded by protracted legal fights between the proponents of the RCA group and the advocates of the competing CBS (Columbia Broadcasting System) television system (Roman, 1967, p. 48).

The French system, SECAM (Séquential à Mémoire), developed between 1958 and 1960, was the brainchild of Henri de France (Roman, 1967, p. 148). He had been the owner of an electronics company that went out of business. A pioneer of many advances in the history of television, he was also a controversial figure as the leading advocate for the 819-lines standard with monochrome television. The O.R.T.F. (Organisation de Radiodiffusion et Télévision Francaise), as well as other companies and organizations, experienced so many technical problems in broadcast exchanges caused by the difference of lines standards between France and the Continent, that a new decision was reached to adopt the Continental standard of 625 lines with color television. However, Henri de France was remembered somewhat bitterly by the opponents of the 819-lines standard, both in France and abroad.[1]

The patent rights to the SECAM color television system were acquired by Maurice Ponte, a French scientist who was also president of Compagnie Télégraphie Sans Fils (CSF). Ponte arranged the formation of a new company, Compagnie Francaise de Télévision (CFT), to handle the SECAM patent. Although Maurice Ponte was the dynamic force behind both companies, ownership of CFT originally was divided equally between CSF and Saint-Gobain, a glass manufacturing company. In the mid-1960s the French government and the Floriat conglomerate bought an equal share of CFT as well, thus giving each partner a 25-percent ownership.

The German system, PAL (Phase Alternation by line), was conceived and developed by Dr. Walter Bruch of AEG-Telefunken in 1962 (Bruch, 1969). Based on fundamental patents and ideas of the

[1] The relationship between Henri de France and the O.R.T.F. was said to be filled with difficulties. In the first place, de France had been the author of the unpopular 819-lines standard which O.R.T.F. had fought to change. Second, he was not a graduate of the École Polytechnique. O.R.T.F. was famed for its cadre of highly qualified technical experts who were former "polytechniciens." He was excluded from (and regarded as somewhat of an "upstart inventor" by) this tightly-knit clique. On the Continent, he was disliked by those in broadcasting organizations who resented his role in the monochrome lines-standard controversy. Yet, he was a popular figure in the press, in which his SECAM invention was greeted with widespread enthusiasm. Indeed, his surname "de France" was patriotically prominent whenever SECAM was discussed.

other two systems, PAL arrived on the European scene as a late contender for the color television system sweepstakes. The development of PAL is examined in detail in Chapter 4.

Technical differences between the systems. Ninety-five percent of the components of the NTSC, SECAM, and PAL color television systems are the same (Paulu, 1970, p. 35). The three systems have much in common because they were all based on the fundamental principles of compatible color television, "compatible" in this sense meaning that color signals could be picked up by black-and-white images. In terms of program exchange between the three color television systems, incompatibility existed without the use of transcoding equipment (New British device facilitates U.S. color TV link, 1967; U.S. TV hops to Europe, 1972). It is very important to emphasize that, while the development of transcoding equipment eventually made program exchange between the different systems possible, the equipment at this time was not in operation. In fact, it was two to three years following the 1966 Oslo convention of the C.C.I.R. that this equipment was employed.

In all three systems the luminance (brightness) and chrominance (that property of light producing sensation of color in the eye, apart from any variation of brightness) are transmitted separately. The luminance information is emitted in the form of two chrominance signals modulating a color subcarrier (Hansen, 1964, p. 40).

The significant difference between the three systems lies in the methods of modulating the color subcarrier: the NTSC and PAL systems use AM modulation while the SECAM system uses FM modulation. What happens is that three signals are needed for each line, one luminance and two chrominance signals. In layman's terms, SECAM sends the chrominance signals successively in the form of A, B, A, B, A, B, etc., on alternating lines. Both PAL and NTSC, however, send all the signals for each line successively in the form of A and B, A and B, A and B, etc. PAL differs from NTSC in a periodical alternation from one line to the next of the phase of one of the modulation components (Hansen, 1964, p. 40). SECAM, by using an alternating scheme to send the information, sends less information. Apparently, this does not significantly affect the quality of the picture received by the viewer. This is because a delay line makes it possible to receive the two signals simultaneously. Hence, the names of the systems can be seen to be derivative from their technical operation: PAL (Phase Alternation by Line) and SECAM (Sequential with Memory).

There are other differences between the systems. They are transmitted along different lines standards (PAL and SECAM use 625 lines, NTSC uses 525 lines) and fields. Some of these variations stem from the fact that the NTSC system was chosen several years before a higher lines standard had been perfected. It was too costly to switch the NTSC system from the 525-lines, 60-field pattern to the 625-lines, 50-field pattern used by both PAL and SECAM.

It is not the purpose here to examine in detail the technical differences, superiorities, or flaws of the different color television systems, except as these relate to political and/or economic claims. Furthermore, it is not in the scope of this work to judge or set criteria by which the technical differences may be evaluated. Rather, the focus in the following pages is on the political and economic factors leading to (and the consequences of having) different color television systems. (For researchers interested in lengthier discussions about the technical functioning of the systems, see Theile, 1965; see also Electronic Industries Assn., 1965; Hirsch, 1966; McLean, 1966; Mili, 1973a, p. 125; Parker, 1966; Rennick, 1966.)

COLOR TELEVISION: THE LINES STANDARDS

What Is a Lines Standard?

All television systems, whether black-and-white (monochrome) or color, contain a number of horizontal lines across the screen of a receiving set. Different systems are usually identified by the number of these lines in the picture. The number of lines across the picture is related to the degree of clarity in the image depicted on the screen. When television broadcasting started, little consensus existed regarding the exact number of lines necessary to project the images. This was due in part to the experimental nature of television at that time, to the lack of interest in an integrated Europe, and to the protectionist motivation in carving particular markets for different domestic industries. The number of lines in the standards operating varied from about 405 to 819 (Codding 1959; Hansen, 1966; Paulu, 1970).

"The direct exchange of programs throughout the world," as the British authority George Codding noted, was "hampered by the fact that several varying standards of broadcast definition" were in use (Codding, 1959, p. 129). To illustrate this point, Codding (1959) cited the following facts about monochrome television:

> The United Kingdom alone uses a definition of 405 lines per picture with a bandwidth of 5 Mc/s. At the other extreme is France with a definition of 819 lines per picture and a bandwidth of 14 Mc/s. Using the same standards as France are Luxembourg and Monaco. All the

countries of North and South America, with the exception of Argentina and Venezuela, use a definition of 525 lines and a 6 Mc/s bandwidth. Also employing this standard are Iran, Japan, Korea (Republic of), Philippines, Saudi Arabia and Thailand. Other countries use a picture of 625 lines and 7 Mc/s bandwidth, with the exception of nine in Eastern Europe which employ 625 lines, but with a 8 Mc/s bandwidth rather than one of 7 Mc/s (the nine are Albania, Byelorussian S.S.R., Bulgaria, Czechoslovakia, Hungary, Poland, Rumania, Ukrainian S.S.R., and U.S.S.R.). (Codding, 1959, p. 129; see also Recent work of C.C.I.R. Study Group on Television, 1950, 1951)

At first these lines-standard variations had little effect, except to limit sales of television equipment to countries on the same standards. As television improved, the idea of European integration attracted more attention, and the number of lines in the standards became very important. One way in which the idea of European integration was promoted was through the formation of international television events and international television broadcasting organizations that facilitated the exchange of programs from one country to another. Established with the assistance of national broadcasting organizations in Europe, Eurovision, for example, now serves as a primary clearinghouse in transmitting internationally the exchange of programs, news, events, etc.

While Europe was divided by these numerous lines standards, program exchange was extremely difficult. Programs had to be broadcast and then transmitted through equipment which would enable viewers on different lines standards in different countries to receive them. This procedure was costly, caused time delays, and frequently resulted in inferior technical quality (Paulu, 1970, p. 236; Pulling, 1963, pp. 10-11; see also Emery, 1966; Green, 1972).

According to the E.B.U. *Bulletin,* the differences in standards were more a result of industrial and commercial interests than technical considerations (quoted in Codding, 1959, p. 129). Great Britain was the first nation to transmit regular television programming before World War II and to resume it after the war. Britain decided to retain prewar standards for many reasons. With the equipment on hand, the British could maintain their leadership and stimulate their electronics industry by resuming service as quickly as possible. In the United States, "the post-war television industry wished to take immediate advantage of the new medium's potentialities and being unwilling to await further discussions about definitions, also pressed for adoption of pre-war standards" (Codding, 1959, p. 129; see also Layton, 1972, pp. 118-121; Paulu, 1970, p. 37). In France, however, the choice was dictated "both by the wish to give the public the best possible quality and also, we must admit, to give the national industry, which would not have been able to compete with its powerful rivals on the simple basis of mass production, the new weapon of quality" (Coding, 1959, p. 129).

Initially, the lines-standard differences served to create domestic markets for the sale of television sets. Once these markets started to become saturated in the industrialized West, the difference in lines-standards was viewed as a barrier to trade in foreign markets. As the quality of television programming improved, a new market developed to export quality television programs. Consequently, a movement developed within the national and international broadcasting organizations to eliminate transmission problems and settle upon a single lines-standard. The opportune moment was identified as corresponding to the establishment of color television broadcasting. The choice of a lines-standard for color television was regarded as the chance to rectify the mistakes of the past and charter a new course for the future. That course was to be one of unity. The lines-standard would be 625 (Business abroad: A rosy hue, 1966, p. 95).

The Difference Between a Color Television System Standard and a Lines-Standard Definition

The number of lines used by a television system can be established independently of the type of system chosen for monochrome or color broadcasting. Although it was argued that the American color television system was geared to 525 lines, it was technically feasible to transmit the NTSC system on other lines-standards. Both PAL and SECAM use the 625-lines standard, yet program exchange between the two systems is not possible without transcoding devices or special multistandard sets. Multistandard sets, capable of receiving broadcasts from different systems or different lines standards are still extraordinarily expensive (Hansen, 1966, p. 138; Hirsch, 1968).[2] Most countries eventually agreed to establish a 625-lines standard and old lines standards (such as the 405- and 819-lines, in Britain and France, respectively) are gradually becoming obsolete (Business abroad: A rosy hue, 1966, p. 95).

[2]See also Beadle (1963, p. 133), on the "twin problems" of choosing a color television system and defining a lines standard. Beadle's book clarifies the difference between the two problems and why they are often confused. Herbstreit and Pouliquen (1967, p. 22), warned of the high cost of multistandard sets:

Multistandard monochrome receivers have been found to cost the television viewers up to about 130% the cost of a single standard receiver. Multistandard colour receivers may be expected to have perhaps even a greater additional cost.

COLOR TELEVISION: BROADCASTING

Technical Compatibility

Broadcasting is affected by two major factors: the technical operation of the system and international regulations regarding its use. Although these factors are independent of each other, standardization on both levels is a necessary condition for the system to work. Or, when standardization may not be possible, there must be some device ensuring the technical "compatibility" of one system with a different one.

A television system is said to be compatible with another television system when the signals from one system can be received and accurately reproduced on another system's sets. Compatibility has two aspects. First, it is the property of a color television system which "enables existing black-and-white sets to receive the color signal and produce from it an equivalent black-and-white picture" (Roman, 1967, p. 37; see also Geren, 1965, p. 597).[3] Second, it is the ability to transmit color television signals from one system to a different color television system's sets. Thus, compatibility is a key feature in a television system.

Compatibility must be achieved across many dimensions simultaneously. This includes several variables which are essential, but extraneous to the hardware of the system. Television, like radio, requires consensus on standards, spectrum space, channels, and frequency limits of each channel. The allocation of spectrum space and channels occurred before television was widespread. Consequently, agreement was more easily reached (Codding, 1952, p. 97; see also Paulu, 1970, p. 33). Although these technical issues have involved controversial political and economic questions, the focus of this study is on the setting of standards in color television systems, and the scope is necessarily limited to deal with issues directly pertaining to it.

Perhaps the most fascinating detail in the case of the three competing color television systems is that the controversy centers around a very small difference. Ninety-five percent of the three systems is based on the original American patent rights. The most recent system of the three, the German one, is partially based on French patents. This illustrates how small technical differences in

---

[3]In May, 1967, West Germany's Telefunken introduced a color transcoding device to convert SECAM signals into PAL signals without loss of picture quality. Thus, the problem of incompatibility between the two systems proved less divisive than first appeared to be the case as reported in *Electronics,* June 13, 1966 (Newsletter from abroad, 1967).

the design of a technology may have important political and economic repercussions.

The International Regulatory System: The Arena and the Responsibilities

The international regulations formulated to set standards in broadcast communications are handled by suborganizations of the International Telecommunications Union (I.T.U.). The standards for color television systems were the responsibility of the International Radio Consultative Committee (C.C.I.R.). The task of defining the system of color television to be adopted in Europe fell to Study Group XI of the C.C.I.R. In conjunction with the European Broadcasting Union (E.B.U.), an ad hoc group was formed in November, 1962, to compare the several television systems.[4]

The group was composed of specialists from the E.B.U.-associated Telecommunication Administrations and radio and television manufacturers representing France, West Germany, Italy, the Netherlands, Switzerland, and the United Kingdom. Twenty subgroups were then delegated to study general characteristics, receivers, propagation, transmitting equipment, program-distribution networks, and studio and recording equipment. Based on the results of numerous technical studies which they conducted under all types of conditions, the E.B.U. ad hoc groups then drafted a report with proposed standards for European color television and submitted it to the C.C.I.R. (European Broadcasting Union, 1966).

The report did not cite one of the existing technical color television systems as superior to the others. Rather, it delineated the characteristics which defined the best system. Since each system shared some of the characteristics (while lacking others), the E.B.U. report did not, in effect, judge between them. It was oriented to an evaluation of the systems, "taking into account the various factors which may affect the quality of the color pictures and of the black-and-white compatible pictures, or which may have an effect on the cost of the receivers, their ease of tuning, stability in operation, etc." (Hansen, 1964, p. 40). Thus, the report stated that, under given conditions, one system would work better than the other two, while under changed conditions, one of the other systems might perform more satisfactorily (Hansen, 1964, p. 40).

---

[4] For reports of this ad hoc group, see issues of the *E.B.U. Review—Part A—Technical*, Nos. 77, 80, 81, 84, 87, 88, 89, 91, 92, 93, 95, 96, 97, 98, 99, 104, 109, 110; see also European Broadcasting Union (1966); Nicotera (1964); Pouliquen (1973); Technical cooperation (1973).

It was not the responsibility of these groups to settle the question of patent rights and royalties. On the contrary, the questions of licenses and royalty rights were manipulated by the companies owning the technical patent rights of the systems. The companies involved were: in America, RCA and Corning Glass; in France, CSF-CFT and Saint-Gobain; and in West Germany, AEG-Telefunken.

From the outset, the scope of the international organizations to set standards was limited. Although the C.C.I.R. and E.B.U. could study and define the best color television system for Europe, neither organization had the international charter to impose either a system or the amount of royalties which could be charged for using it. While these organizations could recommend one color television system as technically superior over another system, they did not have the authority to compel any country to adopt the system against its will. In effect, these organizations could only act in an advisory capacity on this problem.

The result was that conflicting international political and economic interests interceded in debates about color television systems. Representatives to the C.C.I.R. and E.B.U. were generally national, technical broadcasting experts. However, during the color television system debate when each nation voted in favor of one system over another one, the representatives heading the delegations were politicians (Comité consultative des radiocommunications, 1967). Their primary loyalty was not to the international organizations but to the domestic industrial and political interests in the countries from which they came. This conflict eventually made agreement upon a single color television standard impossible. It also led to a split within the French delegation between politicians from the Ministry of Foreign Affairs and the broadcasting experts of the O.R.T.F. during the Vienna C.C.I.R. meeting in 1965.

Some of the problems in setting standards for communications technologies arise from the multitude of international organizations having overlapping responsibilities in establishing those standards (Struglia, 1965). These international organizations are global (I.T.U., I.S.O. [International Organization for Standardization], and I.E.C.), regional (C.E.E. [International Commission on Rules for the Approval of Electrical Equipment], C.E.N. [European Committee on the Coordination of Standards], C.E.N.E.L. [European Electrical Standards Coordinating Committee]) and national (A.F.N.O.R. [Association Francaise de Normalisation], D.N.A. [Deutscher Normenausschus], B.S.I. [British Standards Institution], and A.N.S.I. [American National Standards Institute]) in nature. While the concentration of this study is on the C.C.I.R., which had the primary responsibility to choose the standard for the system of color television, other organizations determined standards for cables, bandwidths, etc., which comprise elements of the system. A discussion of international organizations setting standards for communications technologies will illustrate the numerous problems that exist in attempting to reach agreement on international standards (Crane, 1977).

WORLD ORGANIZATIONS SETTING STANDARDS IN COMMUNICATIONS TECHNOLOGIES

The International Telecommunications Union (I.T.U.)

The International Telecommunications Union, founded in 1865, was one of the first international organizations (Smith, 1969). Its three main purposes are: to maintain and extend international cooperation for the improvement and rational use of telecommunications; to promote the development and most efficient operation of technical facilities in order to increase their usefulness and, as far as possible, to make them generally available to the public; and to harmonize the actions of nations in the attainment of these common ends (Wallenstein, 1972, p. 367; see also Fijalkowski, 1965, pp.205-212).

The I.T.U. has six main functions: the allocation of the radio-frequency spectrum; the registration and coordination of radio-frequency assignments to avoid harmful interference between transmitters of different nations; the maintenance of economical charges for telecommunications; the creation, development, and improvement of telecommunications in newly independent or developing countries, especially through participation in the appropriate programs of the United Nations; the adoption of measures for ensuring the safety of life through the cooperation of telecommunication services; the undertaking of studies and data-gathering to publish information for the benefit of the members and associate members of the I.T.U. (Berrada, 1970, p. 641).

The functions of the I.T.U. are accomplished through its organizational structure (see Mili, 1973a, 1973b, 1973c). The supreme organ of the I.T.U. is the Plenipotentiary Conference, convened every five years. The latest charter of the I.T.U., its Convention, is ratified as an international treaty at that time. This serves as the reference of power for the I.T.U.'s Administrative Council which possesses most of the powers of the Plenipotentiary Conference during the five-year intervals between sessions. Telecommunication law has as its source the Convention, supplemented and amplified by the Telegraph, Telephone, Radio and Additional Radio Regulations (Wallenstein, 1972, p. 367). These regulations are the so-called "world's Bible" for the use of the radio-frequency spectrum (Wallenstein, 1972, p. 369).

The four permanent organs of the I.T.U. are: the General Secretariat (this division provides administrative services for the I.T.U., manages a technical assistance program, arranges seminars, publications, etc); the I.F.R.B. (International Frequency Registration Board); the C.C.I.R. (International Radio Consultative Committee); the C.C.I.T.T. (International Telegraph and Telephone Consultative Committee). The I.F.R.B., C.C.I.R., and C.C.I.T.T. will be discussed in more detail in subsequent sections.

In 1947 the I.T.U. entered into an agreement with the United Nations whereby it was recognized as the specialized agency for telecommunications (Wallenstein, 1972, p. 365). There are 144 member nations of the I.T.U. Although it is an intergovernmental organization, it includes not only government authorities but representatives from all bodies interested in telecommunications, such as governmental administrations, national organizations, private operating agencies, industrial undertakings, and scientific groups (Mili, 1973d, p. 128).

Although the activities of the I.T.U. have immense commercial and political implications, it is an organization which is relatively little known to the general public. I.T.U. conferences and meetings are productive. They are conducted in an atmosphere of international cooperation, which may account for their lack of media news-worthiness (Wallenstein, 1972, p. 365). (On the other hand, the political nature of seemingly technical decisions may elude general comprehension.) This emphasis or concentrating on opportunities for agreement is accentuated through three unique features of the I.T.U.

First of all, it is highly unlikely that a conference convened by the I.T.U. can close without reaching concrete conclusions. This is due to the fact that conferences or meetings are never convened until the conditions that will ensure their success appear to have been met (Mili, 1974). This means, for example, that the agenda must first be approved by a majority of the members of the Union (Mili, 1973d, p. 125).

Second, it is the right of every delegation to enter reservations while the conference is proceeding. This enables members to ratify the final acts of the conference without necessarily agreeing to certain provisions (Mili, 1973d, p. 125).

Third, although all members must be given an advance notice of one year prior to a conference, there is no provision requiring a certain quorum to validate the deliberations of the conference: discussions are valid, regardless of the number of accredited delegations attending (Mili, 1973d, p. 125).

The I.T.U. also has a unique financial structure. Members are free to choose the amount of financial support they will furnish, in line with certain classes of contributions. This provision successfully shifts the moral and personal responsibility of support to each member of the I.T.U. (Mili, 1973e, p. 178).

The I.F.R.B. of the I.T.U.

The I.F.R.B. was created in 1947 for the purpose of bringing order to the chaos of the radio spectrum. The duties of the I.F.R.B. are both legal and technical. Consequently, absolute impartiality in fulfilling them is demanded. This is attained through the election of a five-person independent board, which acts "as a corporate body in which the individual members serve as custodians of the international public trust" (Activities of the International Frequency Board, 1973, p. 402). Elected members are chosen to provide wide geographical representation.

The I.F.R.B. is not normally thought of as a standards-setting agency. Yet, its activities in assigning frequencies are closely related. The essential duties of the I.F.R.B. are: the processing of frequency assignment notices received from administrations for recording in the Master International Frequency Register; the coordination of seasonal schedules of high-frequency broadcasting with a view to accommodating requirements of all administrations for that service; the publication of frequency lists reflecting the data recorded in the Master International Frequency Register, as well as other material relating to the assignment and use of frequencies; the review of entries in the Master Frequency Register in order to amend or eliminate those which do not reflect actual frequency usage, as specified in the agreement with the administrations concerned; the long-term study, of the usage of the radio spectrum, in order to make recommendations for its more effective utilization; the investigation, upon request by interested administrations, of harmful interference, in order to formulate recommendations with respect thereto; the provision of assistance in radio spectrum utilization for member administrations; the collection and publication of monitoring observation results; the referral of all technical questions arising from the Board's examination of frequency assignments to the C.C.I.R.; the technical planning for radio conferences (WARCs); the participation in an advisory capacity, upon invitation by the organizations or countries concerned, in conferences and meetings at which questions relating to the assignment and utilization of frequencies are discussed; and the performance of any additional duties concerned with the assignment and utilization of frequencies and prescribed by a competent conference of the Union, or by the Administrative Council (Activities of the International Frequency Board, 1973, p. 402).

The work of the I.F.R.B. entails maintaining close communication with other specialized international organizations with overlapping interests, such as: the International Civil Aviation Organization (I.C.A.O.); the Inter-Governmental Maritime Consultative Organization (I.M.C.O.); the Asian Broadcasting Union (A.B.U.); the European Broadcasting Union (E.B.U.); the International Radio and Television Organization (O.I.R.T.); and the Union of National Radio and Television Organizations of Africa (U.R.T.N.A.) (Activities of the International Frequency Board, 1973, p. 402).

Technical preparation for conferences is carried out by assembling the necessary data from studies of the I.F.R.B. and these other organizations. At the end of each conference, it is the duty of the I.F.R.B. to prepare letters to administrations, analyzing the decisions of the conference with guidelines for their implementation (Activities of the International Frequency Board, 1973, p. 402). These efforts are made to coordinate and exchange information with the multiple regional and world organizations concerned with the process of the standardization of communications.

The C.C.I.R. of the I.T.U.

The C.C.I.R. was founded in 1927 as the radio communications division of the I.T.U. Since then its scope has broadened to include the study of technical and operating problems of not only radio communications but also television, radioastronomy, and telecommunications via satellite (Pouliquen, 1966, p. 233). Questions pertaining to these areas are examined through the C.C.I.R.'s fourteen Study Groups. These areas cover: transmissions; receivers; fixed service systems; space systems and radioastronomy; propagation over the surface of the earth and through the nonionized regions of the atmosphere; ionospheric propagation; standard frequencies and time signals; international monitoring; radio relay systems; broadcasting; television; tropical broadcasting; mobile services; and vocabulary. In addition, there are two Joint Study Groups with the

C.C.I.T.T. on television transmission and circuit noise. The C.C.I.R. is also engaged in several Joint Working Parties with the C.C.I.T.T. on economic and technical comparison of transmission systems and primary sources of energy; there is also at least one Joint Working Party with the C.C.I.R., C.C.I.T.T., and the I.E.C. (International Electrotechnical Commission) on the standardization of graphical symbols (Pouliquen, 1973, p. 233). Every three years the C.C.I.R. meets in Plenary Assembly to review the work done preceding these sessions. Resolutions are then either dropped or approved as final acts. Participants in the C.C.I.R. are members and associate members of the I.T.U. Upon request, recognized private operating agencies may join the C.C.I.R. The same spirit of international cooperation which pervades the I.T.U. in general is operative also in the C.C.I.R.

This leads to extensive collaboration with international organizations interested in standardization, such as the U.I.R. (International Broadcasting Union), the E.B.U., the O.I.R.T., the U.R.S.I. (International Scientific Radio Union), etc. The C.C.I.R. works in conjunction with these organizations by providing them with questions to study. In this way, information is exchanged and project duplication can be avoided. Furthermore, the C.C.I.R. draws the attention of other international organizations, such as the W.M.O. (World Meteorological Organization), to studies conducted by the C.C.I.R. which are of obvious interest to them. In turn, it draws extensively on their work, particularly that of the I.E.C. (Pouliquen, 1973, p. 233). The C.C.I.R. provides the only world-wide forum for the exchange of technical information and informed opinion in the area of radio telecommunication in its broadest sense.

The C.C.I.R. attempts to integrate a total communications system. Internationally, the I.S.O. (International Organization for Standardization) and the I.E.C. (International Electrotechnical Commission) handle, in general, only specific sections of complex systems. While the I.E.C. may standardize consumer audio-tape characteristics and the I.S.O. may standardize the dimensions of photographic motion picture film, the C.C.I.R. is concerned with integrating these isolated efforts into complete communications systems (Pouliquen, 1973, p. 233). It is concerned not only with the dimensions of films intended for television use, but also with the characteristics of the television camera system that will reproduce the film (Pouliquen, 1973, p. 233). In the area of telecommunications, many parts of the world look to the C.C.I.R. for leadership and guidance. Manufacturers intending to sell broadcasting equipment abroad will often be asked to produce bids based on C.C.I.R. standards specifications (Pouliquen, 1973, p. 233).

The C.C.I.T.T. of the I.T.U.

Although the International Telephone Consultative Committee (C.C.I.F.) and the International Telegraph Consultative Committee (C.C.I.T.) had been in existence since 1924, it was not until 1956, under the auspices of the I.T.U., that these two independent organizations were merged into the International Telegraph and Telephone Consultative Committee (C.C.I.T.T.) (Valensi, 1965, p. 14). The purpose of the C.C.I.T.T. is to study and make recommendations on technical, operating, and tariff questions for the various telecommunications services. Like the C.C.I.R., it also pays attention to the study of questions of particular interest to developing countries (Namurois, 1972, p. 12).

The C.C.I.T.T. sponsors about sixteen Study Groups, eight Joint Working Parties, and several special groups. Study Groups of the C.C.I.T.T. are concerned with: telegraph and telephone operations and tariffs; general tariff principles; maintenance of the international network; protection against electromagnetic disturbances; protection of cable sheaths and poles; definitions, vocabulary, and symbols; telegraph apparatus, transmissions, and switching; telephone switching and transmission performance; semiautomatic and automatic telephone networks; facsimile; transmission systems; telephone circuits; and data transmission (United Nations, 1968, p. 535).

In both the C.C.I.R. and the C.C.I.T.T., the agreed-upon recommendations do not have the status of a treaty. However, because of the provisions made for compromise and cooperation in the I.T.U., the recommendations generally have unanimous approval. Moreover, they are widely followed by member administrations (Gould, 1971, p. 40). Each country has national C.C.I.R. and C.C.I.T.T. organizations through which activities are coordinated. As in the case of the C.C.I.R., extensive international cooperation and collaboration are strongly encouraged. Many of the same organizations operate in conjunction with both consultative committees. The work of the C.C.I.T.T. concerns the nonradio aspects of the telephone, telegraph, data, and video services. There are areas of overlapping interests with the C.C.I.R. which are handled through joint working groups. The C.C.I.T.T. has the additional responsibilities of determining tariffs, as well as managing the World and Regional Plan Committees (Wallenstein, 1972, pp. 367-368).

The pursuits of the C.C.I.T.T. are complicated by the existence of multiple regional standardizing organizations which often promulgate conflicting standards. Since these organizations are responsible for large geographical areas, once they have adopted particular standards prior to recommendations of the C.C.I.T.T., it becomes extremely difficult to ensure world-wide compatibility. The types of regional organizations of special importance in this domain include: the Bell System of North America, the Conference of European Postal and Telecommunications Administrations (C.E.P.T.) for most of Europe, the African Postal and Telecommunications Union (A.P.T.U.), the African and Malagasy Postal and Telecommunications Union (U.A.M.P.T.), and the Inter-American Telecommunication Conference for Latin America (C.I.T.E.L.).

Considerable concern has been expressed in North America that efforts should be directed towards enforcing compatible standards between the Bell System and the I.T.U. Since the rest of the world tends to use C.C.I.T.T. standards, the United States is cut off from the world telephone equipment market. There is pressure from American industry for federal support to achieve the compatibility (Industry asks federal export aid, 1972, p. 54).

The consultative committees encounter logistics problems in their working parties. These stem from the time restrictions, availability of technical experts, the numbers of participants with legitimate interests in the proceedings, etc. Moreover, language differences pose problems when so many people are working closely over technical issues.

International Organization for Standardization (I.S.O.) and the International Electrotechnical Commission (I.E.C.)

In the field of international standardization, there are two predominant world-standardizing bodies, the International Organization for Standardization (I.S.O.) and the International Electrotechnical Commission (I.E.C.). Their work has an influential impact on standards decisions in the field of communications. Since they are affiliated organizations, they will be discussed together.

In the early 1920s, several European nations had established national standards organizations. By 1926 the International Federation of National Standardizing Associations (I.S.A.) was formed to facilitate cooperative work between the various national standards institutes and help them develop national acceptance (Ainsworth, 1964, pp. 364-365). The activities of the I.S.A. were interrupted by World War II. However, the war provided a significant impetus to the advancement of standardization by forcibly impressing the value of standardization upon those engaged in the procurement of war materiel. Immediately following the war in 1954, the International Organization for Standardization (I.S.O.) was created from the defunct I.S.A. (Ainsworth, 1964, pp. 364-365).

The purpose of the I.S.O. was "to promote the development of standards in the world with a view to facilitating the international exchange of goods and services," and to develop "mutual cooperation in intellectual, scientific, technological, and economic activity" (Podolsky, 1968, p. 44; see also International Standards Organization, 1971). Whereas members of the I.S.A. had encountered problems primarily of national acceptance and understanding, members of the I.S.O. were challenged by problems of expansion and growth from the demand for standardization (Ainsworth, 1964, p. 366).

The most important international standards organization in the field of electrical and electronics products is the International Electrotechnical Commission (I.E.C.), which became affiliated with the I.S.O. in 1947 as its electrical standardizing division, even though it had been in existence since 1904, developing and approving electrical standards or recommendations in its own right. The I.E.C. maintains financial and technical autonomy from the I.S.O.

Both the I.S.O. and I.E.C., in contrast to the I.T.U., are private, voluntary, nongovernmental organizations. Membership in them is not comprised of governments per se. Rather, members of the I.S.O. are the national standards institutes of different countries. Membership in the I.E.C. is granted also to special national committees. In accordance with I.E.C. regulations, these committees have been constituted in "the manner most appropriate to enable them to express their views on the questions under study" (Hoffman, 1963, p. 186). I.E.C. membership is composed primarily of representatives of different national, technical, and scientific bodies interested in the problems of standardization in the electrotechnical field. I.E.C. activities are coordinated between its national committees and national standards institutes. Together, the membership bodies of the I.S.O. and I.E.C. represent nations having 80 percent of the world's population (Podolsky, 1968, p. 44). Their financial support is derived through contributions from private industry and national standards organizations.

The I.S.O. and I.E.C. possess consultative status with the United Nations. This status is important in encouraging United Nations' related organizations to utilize I.S.O. and I.E.C. recommendations in their activities (Ainsworth, 1964, p. 366). The I.E.C. and I.S.O. function through national standards committees which serve as international coordinating agencies by establishing liaison relationships with other international organizations, such as the I.T.U. As mentioned earlier, there are several joint working parties between these organizations. In the capacity of coordinating agencies, they operate as the basic international clearinghouses for standards (Ainsworth, 1964, p. 366).

Neither the I.E.C. nor the I.S.O. publishes standards in the accepted sense of the world. To publish conventional standards would require unanimous approval from all members. Inasmuch as unanimity is virtually impossible for them to obtain, the I.S.O. and the I.E.C. issue recommendations in lieu of standards. A recommendation comes into effect when at least 60 percent of the participating nations vote affirmatively on it (Ewert, 1969, p. 48).

The success of these organizations is limited by the fact that no member nation is obligated to enforce their recommendations (Hoffman, 1963, pp. 196-197). Each nation must consider how the interests of its own industries and people are best served. With the expansion of international trade, the actions of the I.E.C. and I.S.O. are becoming increasingly influential. It has been claimed that:

> It is probably true that no large contract in the electrical or electronics industries is nowadays started without the relevant I.E.C. publications having at least been consulted at some stage of the negotiations. (Ruppert & Stanford, 1967, p. 263)

Technical committees of the I.E.C. are engaged in issuing standards recommendations in areas affecting communications. These committees study: cables, wires, and waveguides for telecommunications equipment; digital data transmission; the reliability of electronic components; electronic tubes and valves; capacitors and resistors for electronic equipment; sound recording; insulation coordination; and electro-acoustics (Hoffman, 1964, p. 228). As pointed out earlier, whereas the I.T.U. divisions deal with complete communication systems as well as their components, the I.S.O. and I.E.C. are concerned only with specific parts of those systems.

The effectiveness of the recommendations of such committees is curtailed by other factors besides those of enforcement and protectionism. Standards recommendations from these organizations cannot keep pace with the intensifying demand for them. Intended to reflect the most recent advances in science and technology, the standards cannot be produced quickly enough. One author contemplating the seriousness of this situation estimated that the I.E.C. publishes only about 130 recommendations every two years, a rate he declaimed as "scandalously slow" (Grove, 1966, p. 97). It seems valid to question the effectiveness of such organizations under the circumstances.

REGIONAL ORGANIZATIONS SETTING STANDARDS IN COMMUNICATIONS TECHNOLOGIES

The International Commission on Rules for the Approval of Electrical Equipment (C.E.E.)

The International Commission on Rules for the Approval of Electrical Equipment (C.E.E.) is considered by many standards experts to be "one of the most powerful code-making organizations in the world" (Price, 1966b, p. 237). The C.E.E. has two basic objectives: (1) the development of safety specifications for electrical products to safeguard the public against electrical accidents and fire; and (2) to achieve uniformity of regulations in separate member countries (Price, 1966a, p. 208).

The C.E.E. accomplishes most of its work through technical committees concerned with: electric wire and cable; rubber insulated flexible cords; thermoplastic insulated cables and flexible cords; plugs, socket outlets, and switches; wire connectors; conduit and fittings; television-receiving apparatus; fuses; switches; miniature circuit breakers; connectors; and mains-operated electronic equipment (Price, 1966a, p. 208). C.E.E. specifications for electronic components are utilized in the communications industry in Europe.

Members of the C.E.E. are the national standards organizations of several European countries. The United States is not a member, because it may not enter into an agreement which approves or accepts the development of standards designed primarily for European use. There are too many differences between the continents on fundamental utilization of voltages and frequencies for this to be possible (Price, 1966a, p. 208). Moreover, there is no single authority in the United States which can enter into an agreement with the C.E.E. to accept foreign-produced goods for sale and use in this country.

In the United States there are over 3,500 electrical inspection agencies, each having responsibility and authority within its jurisdiction to accept or reject products. There is no legal obligation for these agencies to approve products bearing the Underwriters' Laboratories' (U.L.) labels. (Broadly speaking, the C.E.E. and U.L. handle similar types of products.) If foreign manufacturers had their products labeled with the U.S. seal, there is no single authority in the United States which could guarantee country-wide acceptance of the products (Price, 1966a, p. 208).

Europeans regard the fact that there is no single agency with the authority to enforce the adoption standards as a major obstacle to United States' membership in European standardization organizations. In contrast to the United States, most European countries have government-affiliated, national standardization bodies. From the European standpoint, the lack of a corresponding association in the United States is viewed as a problem of assuring that European standards adopted and enforced in Europe would be as rigorously enacted in the United States.

The influence of the C.E.E. is spreading; its specifications are now used as the basis for regulations that control the approval of electrical products for sale, not only throughout Europe but also in many other parts of the world. The I.E.C. refers to C.E.E. specifications, sometimes joining the C.E.E. in solving technical problems.

All these factors pose severe limitations on the effectiveness of competition from the United States. The joint I.E.C.-C.E.E. work in electrical safety has led to opposition from countries outside the C.E.E. orbit, such as India, Israel, Canada, Australia, and the United States. As a result, some of these countries have gained "observer status" in the C.E.E., participating through national I.E.C. committees (Price, 1966a, p. 209). The C.E.E. is not a global organization. It is instead a regional association which exerts powerful global influence. It serves as an example of the problems incurred when regional organizations acquire global sway without assuming global obligations. The result is the removal of trade barriers for certain areas and the erection of stronger ones for world-wide standardization.

C.E.N., C.E.N.E.L.E.C., and the Tripartite Accord

The European Committee on the Coordination of Standards (C.E.N.) was organized by representatives of the national standardizing bodies of the European Economic Community (E.E.C.) and the European Free Trade Association (E.F.T.A.) in 1961. The aim of C.E.N. was defined as the establishment of "standards common to the countries of the European Economic Community and those belonging to the European Free Trade Association in order to promote commerce and interchange of services between these countries" (How CEN works to coordinate national standards, 1963).

C.E.N. is composed of a Committee and Secretariat. The Secretariat is permanent and was assigned to the French national standards organization (A.F.N.O.R.), until July, 1975, when it was moved to Brussels to establish closer ties with the E.E.C. and the C.E.N.E.L.E.C. (European Electrical Standards Coordinating Committee) Secretariat. It was decided that I.S.O. recommendations should be used when possible to avoid overlapping fields of activity. C.E.N. provides third-party certification of conformity to standards for the E.E.C. and

E.F.T.A. It is a voluntary service, particularly concerned with non-electrical products, materials, and components. Electrical goods are handled chiefly by C.E.N.E.L.E.C. and to a lesser extent by the Tripartite Committee (Rockwell, 1970, p. 77).

C.E.N.E.L.E.C. was created in January, 1973, from a merger of C.E.N.E.L. and C.E.N.E.L.C.O.M. (European Electrical Standards Coordinating Committee of the Common Market) in order to have only one European organization in the Common Market dealing with the harmonization of standards of electronic and electrical goods. The Tripartite Committee acts as the executive delegate body of the thirteen countries in the E.E.C. and E.F.T.A. It is composed of representatives of governmental and standardization agencies from the Federal Republic of Germany, France, and the United Kingdom. Its work is not restricted to electrical and electronics products.

In the particular field of electronic components, both C.E.N.E.L.E.C. and the Tripartite Committee have aimed at facilitating international exchange through setting up a "harmonized system" known as the C.E.C.C. (the C.E.N.E.L. Electronic Components Committee) system. The C.E.C.C. is intended to unify specifications and quality assurance (Q.A.) inspection procedures (European components standards accord, 1970). Through the C.E.C.C. there is a mutual recognition of Q.A. among the participating countries. Electronic components can cross national borders without further testing, provided that the goods were manufactured by a member country and were certified by the specified organizations of that country as having met mutually agreed-upon standards. Products from nonmember countries, however, may have to undergo additional, expensive, and prolonged testing (Restrictive effects of industrial standards, 1972, p. 615).

Both organizations operate in conjunction with the I.E.C. and C.E.E. in eliminating technical barriers to trade among the participating nations. Yet, the formation of these organizations may be restrictive in terms of global harmonization of standards in communications. The expensive, time-consuming procedure of certification for products of nonparticipating nations is a limitation on international commerce. Even when there is no technical disparity between the products of nonmember countries and members of C.E.E., C.E.N.E.L.E.C., and the Tripartite Committee, the lack of recognized testing facilities may act as a deterrent to trade (Rockwell, 1970, p. 78).

This is especially true for the United States which had for some time expressed the desire to join, but as a non-European country, could not. Discussions on the subject of a possible association with the United States were held at an intergovernmental conference in London in June, 1971. Although it was generally agreed that association with such a major producer of electronic goods might prove beneficial, conditions did not exist at that time to permit such a move. In particular, the United States did not possess an adequate nation-wide Quality Assurance organization. It was recognized in London that a possible solution lay in the development of a world-wide Q.A. system for electronic components which the United States could join. The I.E.C. has agreed to undertake the building of this system.

Meanwhile, the formation of regional organizations may undermine the competitive position of the United States and pose several grave questions for the future. First, to what extent do these accords represent European predilections for similar agreements in other fields? Second, can the formation of other regional blocs such as C.O.P.A.N.T. (Pan-American Standards Commission) be controlled so that global and not just regional standards can be developed? The answers, in turn, will depend on several factors, not the least of which will be the ability of the regional organizations to coordinate and survive.

NATIONAL ORGANIZATIONS SETTING STANDARDS IN COMMUNICATIONS TECHNOLOGIES

A.F.N.O.R., D.N.A., B.S.I., and A.N.S.I.

A.F.N.O.R. (Association Francaise de Normalisation) is the official standardizing agency in France. Founded in 1926, A.F.N.O.R. is a private organization which enjoys official status in its work (Birle, 1961, p. 106). A.F.N.O.R. operates in conjunction with the U.T.E. (Union Technique de l'Électricité), which handles standardization in the electrical and electronics fields (Bachélard, 1972, pp. 26-30; see also Durand & Frontard, 1972). Whereas French participation in the international activities of I.S.O. is directed through A.F.N.O.R., the U.T.E. is closely associated with the I.E.C.

Standardization is a two-step process in France. Through A.F.N.O.R. or the U.T.E., draft standards are drawn up and disseminated. Amended draft standards are then submitted to the Commissioner for standards (Commissaire à Normalisation). From the Commissioner the draft standard is circulated to other government departments for ministerial ratification as a French standard. All departments are then obligated to apply the standard, although the standard is not mandatory in private transactions (Birle, 1961, p. 107). Another feature of French standardization is the "N.F. Mark." The purpose of this mark is to certify that products bearing the N.F. notation comply with the conditions laid down by the standard. Management of the N.F. mark is controlled through A.F.N.O.R. It is financed through dues paid by holders of the N.F. mark license (Birle, 1961, p. 108).

D.N.A. (Deutcher Normenausschus) is the German Standards Association. Organized in 1917, the D.N.A. establishes standards in all fields of science and technology, except for safety for electrical engineering. These are issued by the Verband Deutscher Elektrotechniker (V.D.E.). In the international realm, the V.D.E. participates in the work of the I.E.C., and the D.N.A. is a member body of the I.S.O. (Bachélard, 1974, p. 111). D.N.A. is a nonprofit organization which is financed through membership dues and sales of standards (D.I.N.) and booklets dealing with standardization. In West Germany, the use of standards is voluntary, except for those cited in government regulations. Uniformity of German standards is achieved through special divisions of the D.N.A. (Zinzen, 1963, p. 366).

B.S.I. (the British Standards Institution) issued British standards (B.S.) for the first time in 1901 (Woodward, 1972, p. v.). Unlike its counterparts, the A.F.N.O.R. and D.N.A. in France and West Germany, respectively, the B.S.I. formulates all standards in Great Britain, including those pertaining to electrical safety and electronics. A private organization endowed by a royal charter, the B.S.I. also receives financing through sales of standards and from subscriptions of members (Bachélard, 1974, p. 11). The spirit of standardization in the B.S.I. is characterized by a strong sense of independence from government control. Standards are developed through extensive research, building upon as broad a consensus as possible. Yet, standardization in Great Britain is hampered by sometimes conflicting desires. On one side, the British do not want to standardize too differently from what is practiced in the United States; on the other, they wish to remain part of the European cadre (Bachélard, 1974, pp. 31-32).

A.N.S.I. is the American National Standards Institute (Froste, 1962; Lamb, 1962). In contrast to many European countries, the United States has a decentralized system of developing standards (How we use ASA, 1964; Introducing the USA Standards Institute, 1966). Hundreds of voluntary, trade, technical, professional, and labor organizations, as well as government agencies and departments, may play a role in the generation of standards (USASI's foreign service to industry, 1968). A.N.S.I. is a private organization through which all types of standards are coordinated. A.N.S.I. standards do not have government status (La Que, 1969, p. 144; see also Friesth, 1970, p. 94). But A.N.S.I. does license manufacturers to use its mark on products which have been tested independently and conform to American national standards. Participation in international standards organizations such as I.E.C. and I.S.O. is directed in the United States through A.N.S.I. Yet, this participation is minimal, compared to the activities of A.F.N.O.R., D.N.A., and B.S.I. in international standardization. Standards recommended by major global and regional organizations are adopted in many parts of the world.

This is important, in that international standards are frequently different from those in use in the United States, but the United States has shown only moderate interest in developing international standards. It is possible that the United States may be eventually isolated with unique standards by not participating more actively in international standard-setting. Ultimately, this course may have serious consequences regarding both the American ability to communicate world-wide and the possibility of establishing global standards.

3

*The Development
of a French Policy
to Create
a Color Television Industry*

> The French state has a well-founded reputation for authoritarianism going back to Colbert and the First Empire. It was that characteristic of authoritarianism which permitted an English observer of French life to refer to the domination in France of a "statist tradition." This tradition has been characterized by economic interventionism and by a resistance to the free play of market forces. It has also been marked . . . by the affirmation of the superiority of the state over other economic entities in the determination of the general interest. (Michalet, 1974, p. 107)

A RATIONALE FOR ACTION:
JUSTIFYING "NATIONAL CHAMPIONS"

The Statist Tradition in France

"Mixed enterprise" (the partnership of public and private capital) first attracted widespread attention during the period following World War I, when it was used as a technique to stimulate French industrial sectors not attracting private capital investments (Shonfield, 1965, pp. 82-87). This concept had its roots in the tradition of French mercantilism—the protectionism and enlightened state interventionism inherited from the "ancien regime" (Landes, 1969; see also Hoffmann, 1963).

The state traditionally has been both protector and entrepreneur in France, expected not only to intervene but to assume responsibility for leadership in economic affairs (Shonfield, 1965, p. 86; see also Baum, 1958; Harlow, 1966; Vernon, 1974). However, the success of some governmental policies in areas such as technological development has often been questionable. Millions of francs frequently have been expended on projects which have realized neither substantial profits nor other returns justifying their onerous costs. Yet, in the case of the SECAM color television system, the French did succeed in creating an industry. The benefits of this technology have been political as well as economic in international affairs. It has been a successful "national champion."

The "Technology Gap" and the Development of National Champions

In the French view, the creation and development of independent sources of technology were critical to the maintenance of national independence. It was a question of adapting to the "contemporary scientific technological revolution" or else risking "economic and political subjugation by the world's foremost scientific power, the United States" (Gilpin, 1968, p. 36; see also Nelson, 1971).

In *The American Challenge (Le Défi Américain,* 1967), Jean-Jacques Servan-Schreiber warned that Europe was in a period of economic decline (see also Will Europe face the American challenge, 1972, p. 62). He argued that the Continent would become a subsidiary of the United States, if European countries did not integrate their economies and resources more effectively (Scherer, 1970, p. 347).[5] For the French, economic and technological dependence upon the United States portended a threat to their national survival and independence. They believed that a strong and independent economy was essential to France's maintenance of these goals (Gilpin, 1968, pp. 13-14). Economic invasion by the United States was seen as a "clear and present danger":

> American economic power, the dynamic power of its big businesses and the size of their investments in Europe are the beginning of the colonization of our economy. (Servan-Schreiber, 1967, p. 38)

[5] Evidence supporting this argument can be found in statistics on the estimated dollars exchanged between the two continents in the early 1960s for royalty rights, technical assistance, etc. For example, in 1961 Europeans paid an estimated $250 million to the U.S. for patents, licenses, technical assistance, etc. In return, they received from American firms only about $45 million for the use of technology originating in Europe. Since it was not possible to verify the validity of these figures, and to know what they included, what they purported to measure, or whether they were consistently applied from country to country, it is recommended that they be used with caution as gross estimates.

It was a French ambition to become the scientific-technological leader of western Europe and large areas of the non-Western world. The American superiority in strategic technologies such as computers, aerospace, and atomic energy was distressing to the French and other Europeans, because these technologies were perceived as basic to industrial-military power in the contemporary world. These areas constituted the growth sectors of modern industrial economy and were among the foremost expressions of military power. The French feared that, in an era in which technological innovation is the outcome of scientific research, the "science" or "technology gap" would ultimately lead "to the permanent dependence of Europe on the United States for the technologies required for economic growth, public health and national security" (Gilpin, 1968, pp. 17-19).

The question of whether a "technology gap" actually existed (or exists) is a much debated issue (Gilpin, 1968, pp. 57-76; 1970, pp. 445-448; see also Nelson, 1968). Its importance, however, is its contribution as a rationale for action. As expressed by Robert Gilpin (1968):

> Even if one were to dismiss the existence of any technology gap outside certain militarily relevant areas and to discount the commercial significance of the gap that may exist, vital considerations will remain. *What is important to remember is the political meaning of the technology gap for the French and Europe.* In politics the most important factors are frequently *what people think is true* and the assumptions on which they act, even though the truth of the matter may be something else entirely. (p. 75)

The consequence of these beliefs has been a French policy to create and develop a strong indigenous capability in certain highly advanced technologies that spearhead the industries involved. The history of France has been a history of technological innovation and technological spectaculars, of "nouvelles cathédrales" (Vichney, 1974). These technologies are often referred to as "national champions" and include the fastest plane (the Concorde); the most luxurious liner (the *Ile de France*); the largest solar energy furnace; the first tidal power plant; the most powerful electronic microscope and laser; one of the best color television systems (SECAM); nuclear centers of graphite gas; uranium enrichment facilities; and atomic submarines. In each case the objective has been the same: the French have attempted to excel in certain areas of technology through an enormous investment of resources. During and since the De Gaulle administration, large-scale technological developments—which epitomized the glory, prestige, and independence of France—were heavily funded at huge costs, both economic and political. These grand technological schemes have rarely materialized as anticipated by their visionaries. Some technologies have been developed at a loss of billions of dollars. Other projects have still to show any profit. A few other technologies have been the root of French political isolation or embarrassment in Europe. All the failures have led some to question openly the value of continuing to follow this expensive policy (Vichney, 1974).

PROBLEMS AFFECTING GOVERNMENTAL ACTION

General Problems Hindering the Success of "National Champions"

In the 1950s, foreign observers regarded France as "the most highly protected and most cartelized society among the advanced nations of the West" (Shonfield, 1965, p. 74). Eventually, these practices created problems for France in the European Common Market (Graubard, 1963). The advent of the Common Market meant that France could no longer impose a set of import restrictions designed to help the balance of payments or support certain industries when they were in difficulty. Deprived of their traditional means of defense, planners could not promise protection against troublesome foreign competition in their dealings with big business.

Common Market members objected to any sign that some national industries were receiving assistance from fiscal authorities in comparison to their competitors in the European Economic Community (Shonfield, 1965, p. 133). The opening of the E.E.C. and the restriction or abolition of some of the main policy instruments, such as tariffs, on which national governments had previously relied, caused concern among Common Market nations attempting to rebuild their economies (See Hoffman, 1963). In France the threat of competitive imported products resulted in considerable tension. Several French industrial enterprises had been left in a weakened market position as a consequence of World War II. Different ways to protect French industry and allow it to strengthen its competitive position needed to be found (Holland, 1974, p. 41).

The Problem of Nontariff Barriers

In the elimination of trade protectionism, European attention had focused primarily on the elimination of tariffs as barriers to trade. Other impediments to trade were either "not apparent or of little consequence when tariff rates were high" (Baldwin, 1970, pp. 1-2). The lowering of tariffs had, "in effect, been like draining a swamp." The lower water level had "revealed all the snags and stumps of nontariff barriers that still had to be cleared away" (Baldwin, 1970, p. 2).

With the reduction of tariffs, different forms of trade protectionism flourished within the boundaries of trade agreements; protectionism could then restrict imports without violating the legality of treaties (Bidwell, 1939; see also Curzon & Curzon, 1970; Hemmendinger, 1964; Kelley, 1967; Malmgren, 1970; Massel, 1965; Patterson, 1966). In particular, nontariff barriers presented definitional problems which made them difficult to identify and therefore to regulate. The terms *nontariff trade barriers* or *nontariff trade distortions* include "not only measures that restrict trade but also such measures as export subsidies and government aids that artificially increase the level of trade" (Baldwin, 1970, p. 2). Unlike tariff barriers, nontariff barriers to trade are embedded in a wide variety of domestic legislation and practices; their effect may be slight or substantial (Metzger, 1974, p. 7).

All regulations of trade (other than ordinary rates of duty on ordinary classifications of articles) can be considered nontariff barriers to the extent that they can be, or are, used to interdict trade for protectionist purposes and protect domestic industry against competitive imports (Metzger, 1974, p. 7). There is a consensus that while tariffs have become less of an impediment to world trade, "nontariff barriers have taken over as the tools most widely used to either restrict imports or artificially stimulate export" (Anderson, 1976, p. 29).

The National Association of Manufacturers claims that nontariff barriers impede the flow of trade in several ways. Their very existence creates uncertainty for exporters seeking to penetrate foreign markets. Exporters have difficulty in clearly identifying some nontariff barriers and measuring their economic effects. Furthermore, these barriers restrict the free flow of goods and services and discriminate against foreign supply sources (Anderson, 1976, p. 29).

Determining just what constitutes a nontariff barrier is a complex problem. Since nontariff barriers are so ill-defined and can be hidden in a variety of guises, whether or not something is a nontariff barrier may often be a moot question (Should foreign parts be labelled, 1966). For example:

> Are regulations that are imposed for benign reasons of avoiding deception of the public—such as marking of origin of goods or grading of agricultural products—but that are capable of being used for protectionist purposes, barriers to trade? (Metzger, 1974, p. 7)

In an attempt to classify these regulations, the General Agreement on Tariffs and Trade (G.A.T.T.) cited more than 850 nontariff barriers (Anderson, 1976, p. 29).

In the case of the SECAM color television system, the French government followed a policy dominated by the use of technical standards as nontariff barriers to protect French industry. Other nontariff barriers were also employed. For example, the government participated in trade, through domestic assistance, investment, and foreign promotion programs. Without the basic use of standards, it is doubtful that French policy would have succeeded. The other nontariff barriers used can be regarded as supplemental to the critical use of standard differences in developing an industry for color television. The realization that standards could be used as protectionist nontariff barriers to develop French industry was the result of the disastrous policy followed in the computer industry with Compagnie des Machines Bull.

L'Affaire Bull

One of the most important factors leading to the development of a color television industry in France was the outcome of the computer debacle commonly referred to in France as "L'Affaire Bull." "L'Affaire Bull" was the unsuccessful attempt on the part of the French government to create an independent computer industry, a national champion, which could rival the American giant, IBM.

Compagnie des Machines Bull, after IBM, was the largest computer manufacturer in western Europe. The French had pinned great hopes on the ability of Bull to capture part of the multibillion dollar computer market opening in western Europe. However, Bull was not able to hold its own against IBM. Despite a sales growth from $7 million in 1952 to almost $100 million in 1963, the company found itself in financial, managerial, and technological difficulties Gadonneix, 1974).

> Against the 12 or so computer models IBM had on the market, Bull had one, "Gamma 30," and it was an adaptation of an American computer, the RCA 301, which Bull was manufacturing under license. Nor did Bull have the financial or research capabilities to develop new and more competitive models and the necessary "software." A massive transfusion of computer know-how and risk capital was required. (Gilpin, 1968, pp. 49-50)

To obtain the risk capital and computer know-how, Bull wanted to form an alliance with IBM's American competitor, General Electric. The French government initially rejected G.E.'s bid in 1962 to buy a 20-percent share of Bull. The U.S. government had recently rejected permission for IBM's French subsidiary to sell France computers designed to support the French independent nuclear weapons program known as the "Force de Frappe." The French government was determined to retain control over its single source of computers. Bull was deemed too important to the national defense and France's plans to develop an independent nuclear deterrent to allow affiliation with the American G.E. (Gilpin, 1968, pp. 49-50).

In 1964, when the Compagnie des Machines Bull was in severe financial straits, the French government reversed its position and agreed to an arrangement between Bull and G.E. as a solution to Bull's difficulties. G.E. was permitted to buy 49 percent of Bull. Although "L'Affaire Bull" was primarily a French problem, the drama was watched all over the world. The demise of Bull as an independent French company "served to alert governments everywhere to a fact of economic life which many of them found alarming; this fact was the U.S. domination of the world's computer industry" (Gadonneix, 1974, p. 1).

"L'Affaire Bull" had a profound impact on the European opinion of the technology gap: American corporations appeared to be gaining a stronghold in the strategic growth industries and technological areas most essential to the French economy and national defense. Whether or not any political purpose was involved in their pattern of investment, the threat of U.S. government domination was seen to be there, should the Americans seek to take advantage of the situation (Gilpin, 1968, pp. 50-51).

The French perspective focused on incidents in which the American government had refused to sell France nuclear technology and information made available to Great Britain (The U.S. also refused to sell Great Britain information on communications satellite technology), and on how American firms had been prevented from collaboration with French firms on missile development (Gilpin, 1968, pp. 53-54). By allowing such large holdings of Bull to pass to General Electric, an American firm competing on the world market with another American firm (IBM), the French had allowed "the centers of decision in a vital sector, not only in the economic sense but for the national defense" to be "no longer in France but in the United States" (Gilpin, 1968, p. 55).

"L'Affaire Bull" caused acute concern in France. The French government, under directions "at the very highest levels", appointed a special committee to investigate the circumstances crippling its computer company. They wanted to know where Bull had failed, why, and what could prevent something similar from happening to the rest of the French electronics industry. The investigation led to a series of recommendations for the initiation of an independent electronics industry in France. The proposals specified that the strength of an independent electronics industry in France was critically linked to the French ownership of technology. To be independent of foreign-owned technology, a French company needed to own the license under which it was manufacturing its products. It was noted that foremost among the problems confronting Bull was the fact that Bull was dependent upon an RCA license for manufacturing its main product. By contrast, IBM had about twelve of its own computer models on the European market (Gilpin, 1968, pp. 45-51).

The recommendations focused on the necessity of having sufficient industrial capability to develop the product. In the case of Compagnie des Machines Bull, there was a lack of technical know-how and a dearth of industrial potential to produce a competitive product without foreign assistance, even in software (Gilpin, 1968, pp. 45-51). Perhaps most important of all, "L'Affaire Bull" illustrates the extent to which France required some means of protection for its industry (Schindler, 1964). There was little to "protect" Bull from outside competition. Consequently, Bull was vulnerable to pressures, particularly from the formidable sales efforts not only of its arch rival IBM, but from other American and foreign firms as well. The French concluded that in order to allow a firm to develop a new product, there had to be protection.

In sum, the development of an independent electronics industry in France was found to be dependent upon several factors. Crucial to the success of a company was a French-owned patent, the industrial capability to produce it, and some control of the political, economic, and technical forces in the external environment in order to protect it. Protection of an industry was the key element. It was realized that the SECAM color television system fulfilled these criteria, and standards could be utilized as protectionist nontariff barriers to develop the French industry. The outcome of "L'Affaire Bull" had been to dramatize the possibility of American domination of key sectors of the economy. To the French, SECAM represented one step toward preventing this from happening again.

CHARTERING A NEW COURSE:
THE CASE OF THE SECAM COLOR TELEVISION
SYSTEM

The decision of the French government to promote the SECAM color television system as a "national champion" was motivated by several considerations. Most important of all, SECAM was a French-owned technology. Although SECAM had been based to a large extent on American-owned patents for the NTSC color television system, SECAM was a technical accomplishment of the very highest quality, and many problems existing in earlier versions of NTSC had been eliminated from SECAM.

The development of SECAM was inspired in part as a response to strong pressure from American manufacturers to adopt the NTSC system. While the French appreciated the technological advances achieved by the Americans, in color television at least, they believed there was room for improvement. Unwilling to be "tied like a dog to a leash," the French assumed an attitude that "your solution need not be our solution."

SECAM, as a champion technology, had the potential to project an image of a highly advanced electronics industry, symbolizing for France in electronics what the Concorde represented in aerospace. Political prestige was attached to having a domestic French technology win international adoption. France could gain more global political influence; the standard was not only a technical symbol, but also a political symbol projecting the glory of France. In adopting the SECAM system, other nations would be adopting the French system, rather than the American or German systems.

SECAM signified the potential for the economic independence of France in the realm of this technology. With their own color television system, the French would not be dependent upon another nation, and the French economy would not be inextricably linked with the United States once again. If the French had decided to adopt the existing American color television standard, they would have had to pay royalty fees (at a percentage determined by the Americans) for the license to manufacture NTSC receivers and equipment.

Instead, an anticipated economic return of billions of dollars from world-wide sales of the license rights for the professional and consumer electronics for the SECAM system, as well as the possible market for French color television programs, made the system a lucrative venture.

There was potential economic revenue from royalties, sales of studio, broadcast and transmission equipment, television receiving sets, technical know-how, French movies, entertainment services, etc. The potential market for SECAM in the early 1960s was national and international, including almost every country where the American NTSC had not been established. The potential market excluded only the United States, Canada, and Japan, which had already adopted the American standard (The coming battle, 1966). It did not exclude the potential market for closed circuit television in these countries. It was estimated that by 1980 this market would total at least $12 billion yearly.

Unlike many technologies which the French government supported, the marketable products of SECAM were industrially protected by standards. This was a key reason why the French government believed that SECAM would be profitable; differences in technical standards could be employed as an effective tool to create an industry. Thus, some of the problems encountered in attempts with Compagnie des Machines Bull to develop a computer industry could be avoided in color television.

Finally, the SECAM system presented the French with an opportunity to promote scientific as well as cultural exchanges with other countries. Through the sale of technical know-how, expertise, and television programs, the French had increased possibilities to expand their sphere of influence in other directions. SECAM represented a means of closer cooperation between France and countries adopting the French technology.

President de Gaulle was convinced by the arguments and economic data from his advisers that in the SECAM color television system lay the possibility of a "grande téchnique francaise," a national champion which would surely succeed, because SECAM contained the ingredients that national champions until then had lacked to make France independent of American technology. Combined with the expected lucrative, financial return, these factors prompted President de Gaulle to direct national resources to promote the SECAM system at home and abroad.

The decision to promote SECAM as a national champion was not initially accepted with widespread enthusiasm. For varying reasons the policy was greeted with resistance, both within the electronics industry and in part of the French government itself. If the policy to develop a color television industry were to succeed, these pockets of opposition had to be eliminated and a united stand established. Conflicting political and economic interests arising from (and themselves affecting) the decision to back SECAM had to be controlled. Although conformity could be imposed and enforced internally, other devices had to be utilized to foster the policy beyond French boundaries.

Industrial Opposition to SECAM

The consumer electronics industry in television is dominated by a handful of major corporations in France, although several small companies also manufacture television equipment. During the early 1960s, the companies most concerned with producing color television equipment in France were Thomson Houston-Hotchkiss Brandt, Radiotechnique (Philips's French branch), and CSF/CFT

(Compagnie Générale de Télégraphe Sans Fils/Compagnie Francaise de Télévision) Zysman, 1974).

Unlike the consumer electronics industries in Great Britain and West Germany, French companies felt no immediate pressure to manufacture color television equipment. The French industry could afford to delay producing color sets because their black-and-white television market was still unsaturated. There was agreement in France that the most important issues in the choice of a color television system concerned not haste but the possibility of European unification, the costs involved in manufacturing the system, and the technical performance of the system chosen. Disagreement focused on just which system should be chosen.

French companies wanted to sell as many sets as possible, and the cost of manufacturing the sets was very important to them. Since the French system was heavily based on patents owned by American firms (most notably RCA and Hazeltine), many French companies were worried about the payment for license rights. If the French system were adopted, would this mean that manufacturers would pay twice for the privilege of manufacturing the French system, that is, payments to both the Americans *and* the French patent-holder? Would NTSC offer a cheaper option?

CFT, which had been formed by Maurice Ponte of CSF to produce SECAM equipment, owned the SECAM patent. Therefore, CFT was in a position to gain financially if SECAM were chose. CFT also had the most to lose financially if it were not. Ponte's companies had invested millions of dollars in the development of SECAM. (The exact amount is difficult to determine and estimates vary widely depending on whether or not the cost of the color *tube à grille* is taken into account. A similar situation exists with regard to the investment made by RCA in the NTSC system. According to one source, RCA is rumored to have spent $65 million, by another, $150 million, before a mass market materialized.[6] In addition, CSF was in financial difficulties with the expenses incurred over the development of a French computer industry. Ponte was looking toward SECAM as a sure money-maker to recoup financial losses and investments. If the SECAM color television system were adopted, the SECAM patent would be considered a major asset, should his companies need to engage in a corporate merger.[7] In short, the most

[6] See Scherer (1970, p. 355) and Fight goes worldwide (1964), respectively. Scherer states that the cost of the Xerox 914 copier was about $16 million, and the cost of developing a civilian jet airliner runs about $100 million.

[7] CSF eventually did merge with Thomson to form Thomson-CSF. John Zysman's (1974) thesis explores this merger.

profitable course for CSF and CFT was to encourage the adoption of the SECAM color television system.

The position of CFT regarding the adoption of the SECAM system was not secure, just because SECAM was a French-owned patent. On the contrary, many companies were hostile and openly resented CFT's exclusive patent rights for SECAM. Other companies feared the size of the royalty fees they would be required to pay in order to allow Ponte's companies to recoup their investments and simultaneously make a profit after paying the American licenses. It was said that the SECAM owners would not state the exact amount of royalty fees they would demand. (This was caused by the fact that CSF and CFT had not yet finished negotiating with American firms; it was also a result of the efforts to prolong the choice of the system until SECAM's chances of winning the entire European market were more firmly established.) The lower the royalty fees, the greater was the possibility for other French manufacturers to make a profit.

Other companies were jealous of the prestige accorded CSF and CFT for owning the SECAM patent. CSF was regarded as a company with broad professional, but no commercial, electronics manufacturing experience. It was infuriating to established commercial electronics companies to be excluded from one of the most valuable patents in the history of their industry.

Radiotechnique (Philips's French subsidiary) favored the position of CSF and CFT, opting for SECAM to become the European standard. Traditionally, Radiotechnique had been operating almost independently of its parent company, Philips of Holland. If NTSC were to win, Radiotechnique faced the possibility of being shut down for major economies of scale in production. On the other hand, if differences in national technical standards existed between color television systems, Radiotechnique could justify its existence by manufacturing for the French standard. Thus, Radiotechnique, the major foreign company manufacturing in France, was in the unique position of backing a French technology, while other French-owned companies were reluctant to support their own countrymen.

The French black-and-white television standard had isolated France from the rest of the European continent. French consumer electronics companies sought unification with the rest of Europe through color television; they wanted the system chosen in France to be the system chosen as the European standard. The companies were not convinced that SECAM could effectively challenge the NTSC system for that position. They feared a situation would develop in which France would use the French standard, and every other nation would use the American one. While providing them with a protected domestic market, this situation would be catastrophic to industrial growth because once the French market was saturated, there would be no outlet (i.e., no export market), for French products. Once again, the French would be isolated with their television system.

French companies were anxious that the system chosen should be technically sound, and that it should offer the best technical solution and be amenable to production *en masse*. (Tests officially conducted by the E.B.U. concluded that no single color television system performed at all times and under all conditions in a superior manner to any other system.) Although the French considered the SECAM system to be a technical improvement over NTSC, NTSC had been time-tested. American firms had several years experience producing NTSC equipment. This was important, because the French were as yet unfamiliar with the "bugs" that would occur in manufacturing SECAM equipment on a large scale. In other words, the NTSC system presented an alternative where the flaws were known and had been treated. SECAM was still an unknown product; NTSC was already a proven system.

French industrial dissent was short-lived because of the government's active role in the conciliation process. Through the auspices of F.N.I.E. (Fédération Nationale des Industries Electroniques, the trade association representing the interests of consumer electronics firms), representatives from President de Gaulle arranged to meet with key industrial leaders. The government sought their support for SECAM, and the industrialists were frequently consulted as plans progressed. To assuage wounded egos and jealousies, the government hosted lavish dinners in their honor, appealing to French patriotism and loyalty. Agreement was reached that various companies would conduct "tests" on the SECAM receivers to relieve manufacturers of the fears of technical flaws in this unproven system. Low royalty fees were guaranteed to all French manufacturers as a condition of their acceptance to support the SECAM system. Eventually, governmental policy achieved full industry-wide support. Companies realized it was in their best interests to submerge various jealousies and support the French system. And so the first step toward getting SECAM adopted internationally was successfully completed.

Governmental Opposition to SECAM:
The O.R.T.F.

The degree of authority within an agency to decide on a particular standard may vary from nation to nation. The issues of concern for that agency may not always be similar to other domestic political and economic interests. For example, the French government broadcasting agency, the Organisation de Radiodiffusion et Télévision Francaise (O.R.T.F.) responsible for color television systems, found itself in opposition to the official position adopted by the French government and industry.

Officially responsible for all broadcasting in France, the O.R.T.F. handled technical, commercial, and programming problems. The O.R.T.F. was the governmental arm in broadcasting affairs. It was considered a matter of course within O.R.T.F. that the organization would direct the decision, negotiations, and tests pertaining to color television systems. The abrogation of the right to make the decision created problems within the French technical community, eventually causing a split within the official French delegation at the C.C.I.R. meeting in Vienna in March, 1965. (See Chapter 5.)

The technical problems which arose as a result of the incompatibility between monochrome television standards were discussed in Chapter 2. It was noted there that the difficulties, costs, and frequent delays of program exchanges were particularly annoying to O.R.T.F. technical experts managing international exchanges and transmissions. The technical personnel at O.R.T.F. were strongly in favor of eliminating similar future problems through the installation of compatible color television standards at the outset. In the O.R.T.F. view, the single most important criterion in choosing a color television system was unity with other European countries. Although they intended to select the best technical system, they did not plan to permit political expediencies to govern that choice.

There was some unavoidable hostility at the outset between O.R.T.F. personnel and the inventor of the French system, Henri de France. Critics at O.R.T.F. noted that De France was not a product of the École Polytechnique or the O.R.T.F.; his invention had not been generated in O.R.T.F. laboratories but in industry; he had been the leading advocate of the 819-lines, monochrome standard controversy; and he had some powerful enemies in international broadcasting circles. Thus, his SECAM system was greeted with some resentment and reservations by O.R.T.F., whose experts feared that the rest of Europe would select the proven NTSC system; if the French backed SECAM, they would once again be isolated.

O.R.T.F. engineers performed tests on the different systems in conjunction with the E.B.U. requirements. Their tests did not place SECAM in a significantly superior position to NTSC. As the results of the E.B.U. investigations showed, no single system was found to be better than its competitors, despite numerous studies. O.R.T.F. technical experts wanted to choose a system based on the objective criteria of such tests. Yet, the results of the international studies did not make this goal feasible, based on technical grounds. The O.R.T.F. maintained that the selection of a color television system was the right and function of the O.R.T.F. in France. They bitterly opposed having a decision on a technical question imposed on them by non-technical personnel and based on nonobjective material which ignored problems engendered by the incompatibility of different systems. Yet, this is exactly what occurred. Orders were received from the "very highest levels" of government that O.R.T.F. would support the French SECAM system, regardless of the outcomes of the tests. Politicians had determined the solution to the technical question, rather than the technical experts themselves—politicians, O.R.T.F. engineers argued, who were ignorant of the vast cost and technical ramifications of this decision. Unlike the situation in the electronics industry where hostility gradually disappeared, antagonism increased between O.R.T.F. personnel and French politicians. On the other hand, the state had achieved its plan and obtained the desired end: domestic agreement to adopt the French SECAM system.

4

The Development of an Export Market for SECAM

FRENCH STRATEGY I

The European Approach

The first phase of the French government's efforts to develop a color television industry was completed with the domestic agreement to support SECAM. The next phase was to win international approval for SECAM as the color television standard for Europe in order to obtain revenues for license and royalty rights, and to create an export market for French-manufactured products and technical assistance.

The strategy used by the French in their European campaign for SECAM was twofold. One dimension aimed to discredit the American system technically by presenting it as an inferior product, unacceptable to the demands of most Europeans for high quality (Oganesoff, 1965). The other dimension of the strategy was to market the SECAM technology as the European (versus American) solution, in order to appeal to the shared European fear of overdependence upon American technology. SECAM became known by the American press as France's "Supreme Effort Contra A-merica" (Oganesoff, 1965). The success of this course, however, was dependent upon the continued image in Europe of France as the European David against the American Goliath, with SECAM's position as the only European challenger. The development or intrusion of a second European system would have diminished the effectiveness of this strategy and made it less attractive to other Europeans.

As French and American efforts to display the technical superiority of their respective systems increased, charges and countercharges between the two nations became sharper. Although technical criteria allegedly formed the initial basis for disagreement, as time progressed the fight assumed a more political nature. Supporters for SECAM claimed that it was difficult to use NTSC to record and relay broadcasts over long distances. To rebut this, RCA sent a fully equipped, mobile, transmitting and receiving unit to Europe and to Moscow where the machinery demonstrated color images relayed across 3,700 miles. Not to be outdone, the French also relayed countless tests from Moscow and elsewhere (Oganesoff, 1965; see also Move to promote U.S. system, 1964; RCA in Russia, 1964).

The Americans charged that SECAM was still in a "laboratory stage" and its black-and-white images (for noncolor sets) "would not be found acceptable by viewing audiences either in Europe or anywhere else." SECAM "frequently showed its susceptibility to noise and produced color of inferior quality" (Oganesoff, 1965, p. 10). RCA argued that SECAM sacrificed "long-term flexibility, versatility, performance and cost in favor of correcting short-term problems." The many improvements made in the NTSC system in recent years proved how flexible it was; RCA insisted that SECAM would be costlier to mass produce, because the sets contained more parts than the U.S. mode (Oganesoff, 1965, p. 10).

The French responded that the NTSC system was practically of "horse-and-buggy vintage" in television, that NTSC really stood for "Never Twice the Same Color," while SECAM under difficult conditions was 100 percent reliable (Oganesoff, 1965, p. 10). Because the French system used a superior method of transmission, the sets did not need the hue and intensity controls that were placed on American receivers. To underscore their point, the French promoters of SECAM ran an advertisement in London papers depicting a frustrated viewer angrily twisting knobs of an NTSC set in order to get the colors right. "You have simplified everything in America," said an engineer for CSF, "everything except your color television" (Oganesoff, 1965, p. 10).

SECAM was purported to be immune to the distortions produced by black-and-white video tape recorders and hence could be fed into existing studio equipment instead of the more elaborate recorders needed for the American system. Another economy was that SECAM could be transmitted over long distances through standard unmanned relays while the U.S. system required manually adjusted, more complex, and more expensive relays.[8] Furthermore, the French maintained that SECAM sets could be mass produced at the same price as the NTSC counterparts.

Numerous studies conducted by the E.B.U. showed that no single system was better under all conditions than its competitors, and the average viewer found little difference between the systems. The tremendous advantage for broadcasting by having continent-wide agreement on one system outweighed any slight advantage one system may have had over the other (Paulu, 1970, p. 35; see also Selection of a world-wide NTSC color TV system, 1966; Theile, 1963, 1965).

The German Backlash

While the French and the Americans were struggling to outdo each other with their systems, German industrial representatives sought to negotiate a cross-licensing agreement between A.E.G.-Telefunken and CSF that would include the SECAM patent. Patents protect the engineering designs of the technical operations of color television systems from infringement. The production of equipment for the system by different manufacturers is standardized through complicated licensing agreements of these patents. In turn, the licensees pay the patent-holders a certain percentage of royalties (Scherer, 1970). The percentage paid is determined by several variables, including the relationship of licensee to patent-holder, the number of existing cross-licensing agreements for other patents the two parties have contracted the number of other companies which have the right to produce the same patent, the relative strength of the patent-holding company to the rest of the industry, the amount of time remaining before the patent expires, and the domestic and international laws governing the business operations of the two companies.

Several cross-licensing arrangements had been formed between A.E.G.-Telefunken and CSF in the past. It is common practice for firms in the electronics industry to enter into liasons with foreign companies, and often there is a myriad of complex interconnections among firms. Ironically, two companies which view each other as rivals may be closely allied with a third company. Such was the case

---

[8] This was an important and sensitive area for American manufacturers. In order to sell VTRs, U.S. Department of Commerce export licenses were required but were not forthcoming, until it may have been too late to make a difference for the sale of the American system to the Soviet Union. More attention is given to this topic later in this chapter.

with the firms holding the patent rights for color television systems: both RCA and CSF had agreements with A.E.G.-Telefunken.

It was generally expected in West Germany that CSF would develop the patent for SECAM in conjunction with A.E.G.-Telefunken. This expectation was not unfounded, considering the close degree of association which already existed between the two companies. In addition to several patent exchanges and licenses, both companies had exchanged high-ranking professional employees and technical information since 1956. Previous cross-licensing arrangements between CSF and Telefunken had entailed little or no payment. However, the French were not prepared to give the SECAM patent to the Germans for free. The revenue from the royalties was important to French plans to recoup losses, investments, and finance expansion. Allowing the Germans to manufacture SECAM without financial compensation would have placed the French in a highly disadvantageous position.

It would have meant that industries in both countries would produce equipment for the French standard but that France would not receive any money for these rights from the Germans. Every German sale of SECAM equipment, whether inside Germany or abroad, would be an economic loss for France because France would lose revenue not only from royalties, but from sales of German instead of French equipment. The French were concerned that their own industry would not be able to compete on this basis with the stronger German industry.

They worried that even their domestic market would not provide a guaranteed outlet for French goods because it would be saturated with competitive German electronic products. As members of the European Common Market, the French could not levy tariffs against German equipment to protect the French domestic color television market. The effectiveness of standards as a protection for French industry hinged on forcing the Germans to pay royalties to manufacture for the SECAM standard.

CSF evaded German demands for the free exchange of the SECAM patent in the technically legal claim that the SECAM patent belonged to CFT and not to CSF. Although CSF and CFT were both controlled by the same person, Maurice Ponte, CFT was owned equally at that time by CSF and Saint-Gobain, a glass manufacturing company (Jublin, 1975; see also Erikson, 1966, p. 165). When licensing terms for SECAM could not be satisfactorily concluded with A.E.G.-Telefunken, it was possible for the administrators of CSF to avoid damaging their other technical arrangements with the Germans by blaming Saint-Gobain as the unwilling party to the agreement.

Ostensibly, the issue could not be argued further, since CSF did not fully control the patent and could not be forced to license it under old cross-licensing agreements between Telefunken and CSF.

Until 1960 French engineers in CFT contend that Dr. Bruch of A.E.G.-Telefunken seemed unconvinced that there was a sufficient basis for a common European system. Over the next few years, German opinion radically altered. Two major factors contributed to this change. The first was the French refusal to license SECAM on terms which the Germans regarded as reasonable. The second factor was the German development of a third color television system, the German candidate for the "European solution."

To the extreme chagrin of the French, the German innovation known as PAL (Phase Alternation by Line) was a direct outgrowth of French-owned patents. PAL was basically an ingenious combination of the best features of SECAM (including the delay line), NTSC (particularly the use of AM modulation), and an invention by a CFT engineer, Gerald Melchior, to correct for phase distortion. Using AM modulation (the NTSC standard vs. FM modulation in SECAM) meant that exchange broadcasts between PAL and NTSC would be easier than between SECAM and NTSC. While PAL offered Europeans a system more closely linked to the American standard, it so markedly resembled the SECAM system that French technicians referred to it as a SECAM variation or improved SECAM design.

Dr. Bruch, the inventor of the German system, was allegedly shown the Melchior patent shortly after it had been registered with the French government, but before it became publicly known. Cited in French records as #PV889.835, the Melchior patent was filed on March 2, 1962. Although the patent was effective from that date, under French law it remained unpublished until April 8, 1963. The PAL patent was filed in Germany on December 31, 1962, about nine months after Melchior filed his patent.

The German development meant that there was now a third system competing for the European color television standard, a system from a European country traditionally associated with high-quality technical achievements. PAL could stimultaneously compete on the same basis as SECAM as "the European solution," destroying French marketing strategy while offering the extra advantages of easier exchange with NTSC. Until the development of PAL, the French had operated under the assumption that if SECAM was selected as the European standard, the Germans would adopt and pay for it. Now that the Germans had their own system in the European competition, they had the option of retaining their own system regardless of the system adopted as the European standard.

The French viewed PAL and NTSC as threats to their economic market. If either the German or American systems were chosen as the European standard, the French could lose their chance of building a color television industry. It would lead to the same situation as in giving the Germans SECAM without charge: the French and Germans would share the same standard, but the French would receive no royalty revenues and have no protection from market invasion from the Germans. If one of the other systems were adopted as the European standard and France chose to retain SECAM, the French faced the grim possibility of being isolated in Europe once again.

The French found themselves in an awkward predicament with regard to claiming and obtaining monies for the unauthorized use of French patents in the German system. By the time a company can stop a competitor for violation of its patent rights, the product may already be entrenched on the market. This is not unusual, and examples of such cases abound. For example, nine years ago Xerox sued IBM to prevent IBM from selling a plain paper copier (Polaroid sues Kodak, 1976). The suit is still unresolved. Not only is IBM still selling the copier, but it has since come out with two new ones. In another case, Polaroid sued Kodak to prevent Kodak from entering the instant photography market. At issue, Polaroid contended, were patents infringed by Kodak (Polaroid sues Kodak, 1976). In the case of color television systems, the French decision of whether or not to sue the Germans for patent violations had several other complicating factors.

It is time-consuming and expensive for companies to sue one another internationally over patent royalties. Each time a plaintiff company litigates to gain patent royalties, it must prove that the defendant company is in actuality using those patents and consequently violating patent rights. This must be shown for each alleged violation in every country where patents are being infringed. In addition, the decision reached in a court in one nation does not bind the courts in other countries. There are other political ramifications involved with each decision (Silverstein & Reale, 1973).

Had the French chosen to sue the Germans, in order to prove patent violations they had to sue in a country which had already adopted the PAL system. Since the selection of a color television standard is motivated by several political considerations, it was possible that a country choosing the PAL system was politically inclined toward the Germans. Since each nation had independent powers in its own courts, the French feared a court decision would be colored by political rather than legal factors.

The positions of CFT and Telefunken as promoters of color television systems would have been jeopardized by a trial taking place between them. The percentage of royalties paid on patent rights is flexible. This means that there is an open arena for negotiations and maneuvering of positions. The company holding the patent can demand whatever it believes the market will bear. A trial would have required each company to record publicly information on issues about royalties, technical quality, etc. An out-of-court agreement, however, would protect each company from answering such questions. Each company could continue to promise prospective buyers adopting the system that no extra royalties would be added to the cost of the company's system, that the system under negotiation was technically superior, and so on.

Eventually, CFT administrators reasoned that it was in their best interest to reach an out-of-court settlement with Telefunken. They calculated that such an agreement would ensure them of some economic return, even if it was not as much as originally anticipated. They saw benefits in the prestige to be gained in Telefunken's obligation to inform PAL manufacturers of the royalties being paid to CFT for French patents. It took several years for an agreement to be reached. During the latter part of the 1960s, Telefunken and CFT signed a "nonaggression pact" in which Telefunken agreed to pay CFT a certain percentage of royalties on each PAL set manufactured, approximately 0.75 percent.

FRENCH STRATEGY II

The Russian Partnership

As a result of their failure in the early 1960s to reach an understanding with the Germans, the French altered their strategy of marketing SECAM. It was no longer deemed sufficient to demonstrate SECAM and call it "the European solution," since now there were two "European solutions" and the Germans had equal claim to this title. PAL was considered to have the edge over SECAM; the tradition of high quality of technological products associated with the stronger German electronics industry gave the German system more credibility.

The French realized that they needed support from another country with whom they could promote SECAM for the European standard, or all their plans would be ruined (Business international: The politics of colour, 1965, pp. 691-695). Support had to come from a strong, respected nation where SECAM products could be developed and produced, from a nation whose vote for SECAM would sway the votes of uncommitted and undecided countries in the C.C.I.R. (Mikton, 1963, p. 22).

West Germany and the United States were eliminated as possible partners, because both countries had their own domestic technologies to promote for the European standard in color television (The colour situation, 1965, pp. 130-131). Relations had become somewhat embittered with both countries over this issue. Nor did the French expect that Holland would agree to support SECAM, since the Dutch traditionally supported American or German products. The French turned to Great Britain for assistance in promoting SECAM, and both countries quietly agreed to work together to promote SECAM interests. Before this relationship became widely known, President de Gaulle refused Great Britain entry into the Common Market, and the British canceled plans reached by the B.B.C., O.R.T.F., and both consumer electronics industries.

Locating a partner with whom France could promote the SECAM color television system was critical to French economic and political interests. At stake was the possible loss of the color television market and associated revenue from the SECAM patent, the loss of the opportunity to create an independent color television industry, the possible market invasion in France from German products, the probable dependence upon American and/or German technology, and the blow to French national prestige. The eventual choice of the Soviet Union as a partner was a bold, daring, and desperate maneuver by the French.

From the Russian perspective, the agreement to adopt the French SECAM system reflected foreign policy objectives as well as economic and technical advantages. The Russians had strong political reasons not to adopt either the American or German systems. At this time the Soviet Union and the United States did not encourage the export of, or dependence upon, each other's technology, since each was attempting to assert technological superiority over the other in space, military weapons, etc. Although at least one Russian study in the early 1960s found that the NTSC system of color modulation was technically better, politically it might have been interpreted as a sign of technological weakness for the Russians to install the American system (Zakharov et al., 1964).[9] Furthermore, Russian foreign policy identified West Germany as an imperialist nation; the Russians were not anxious to assist the Germans with a political and economic

---

[9]See Business international: The politics of colour (1965, p. 695): "There are both French and American supporters within the Russian technical camp; but the French have been giving lavish hospitality at a high political level with offers of technical aid to set up the necessary equipment." See also Parrott (1966, pp. 256-257): "At first the Russians seemed interested in the American system, and the supporters of the N.T.S.C. were confident that this would be enough to win the rest of Europe."

buildup by backing PAL. Consequently, the Russians were at the out-set receptive to the idea of adopting the French SECAM system.

No doubt the Russians perceived that an agreement with France on SECAM was a sure way of embarrassing the United States on several levels. The Soviet Union and France might have been gambling that the pressures to conform and agree on one unified system would force both the United States and Germany into accepting SECAM, particularly if the Russians could deliver the eastern European Communist vote, and swing the support of previously uncommitted, Third-World, African, and French-speaking countries. Additionally, there was some hope that West Germany would elect SECAM in order to maintain close communication links with East Germany.

The negotiations between France and Russia over color television were historic political events, marking the first time since World War II that a Western nation agreed to extensive scientific and technological cooperation with the Soviet Union. Charles de Gaulle was the first major Western head of state to visit the Soviet Union, setting a precedent for policies followed in other countries to use cooperation in science and technology as a tool of diplomacy (McElheny, 1966, pp. 43-46).

The scientific and technological exchange between France and Russia began in January, 1964, with the visit to France of Konstantin W. Rudnev, chairman of the State Committee for the Coordination of Scientific Research Work. In October, 1964, Gaston Palewski, the French science minister, returned the visit. During 1965, the first agreement for cooperation on the SECAM color television system was announced. Following that, the Russians and the French increased their collaboration and exchange on space, science, high energy physics, and atomic energy (McElheny, 1966, pp. 43-46).

At the time of the Franco-Soviet accord in 1965, the Russians themselves did not possess a color television system that was sufficiently reliable to enter into C.C.I.R. considerations. The French agreement permitted them to refer to SECAM as the "Franco-Soviet" development, sharing credit for its invention. In this way, it appeared as though the U.S.S.R. had made a significant contribution to the development of color television technology. SECAM offered the Russians a means of gaining prestige in a new field, adding to that already accrued from Russian technological enterprises in space and weaponry.

In eastern European Communist nations, the Russians added a few patented circuits to the system. Some French experts have called these patents "unnecessary." Yet, these patents have enabled the Russians to collect royalties from tangential improvements on a technology (color television) which they had not designed. As further inducement to adopt SECAM, the French permitted the Russians to have the system royalty-free. Some highly placed French government officials account for this French concession as appreciation of a "special relationship" existing between the two nations. Executives of French industry have admitted that the concession was a measure of French desperation to engage a powerful SECAM ally. After all, the issue of royalty fees was the major cause of the rift between the French and German companies in the early 1960s, and the development of a French industry in color television was dependent upon assuring some royalties. By 1965 the PAL system appeared to be gaining favor among west European countries as the choice for the C.C.I.R. standard. Since SECAM's chances of winning an export market were so diminished by PAL's gains, the French were prepared to give their system to the Russians for free to assure that SECAM could compete against its rivals. On an economic level alone, the SECAM agreement was most profitable for the Russians.

The SECAM system was also technically suited to the Russians' broadcasting needs; it was said to be less susceptible to distortion, performing well over long distances. Most important of all, the SECAM system enabled the Russians to use their existing (and already obsolescent) black-and-white video tape recorders (VTRs) and land lines (Parrott, 1966, pp. 256-257; see also Business international: Colour TV: Each to his own, 1965). Ultimately, the issue of VTRs may have played an important role in the Russian decision to back SECAM. It was a fortuitous circumstance for the French that the SECAM system operated with the Russian black-and-white VTRs, for the American NTSC system did not. The NTSC system required the use of special VTRs which had been denied export to Russia. The series of decisions in the U.S. government which eventually permitted their export to Russia may have come too late to win the Russian vote for NTSC.

AMERICAN INFLUENCE ON FRENCH STRATEGY

The VTR Export Controversy

The United States Commerce Department's Interagency Advisory Committee on Export Policy (A.C.E.P.) through its subgroup, the Operating Committee (O.C.), had considered requests from RCA to demonstrate the NTSC system (consisting of a mobile TV studio and TV tape-recorder equipment) in several European and east European Communist countries, including the U.S.S.R. (U.S.

Dept. of Commerce, 1964). In a letter to John Collins, then director of the Division of Scientific and Electronic Equipment at the Department of Commerce, Charles Odorizzi of RCA wrote:

> The French interests promoting SECAM have vigorously attacked the American NTSC standards with irresponsible technical statements and with highly misleading advertising addressed to the general public . . . Nevertheless, the French promoters, by their actions, are creating a climate in Europe which has convinced us that there is a significant chance that the French system could be adopted as the standard for Europe (U.S. Dept. of Commerce, 1964, p. 2).

Odorizzi explained that in the United States alone, color television in 1964 was a billion-dollar-a-year industry (U.S. Dept. of Commerce, 1964, p. 1). In order to demonstrate to the technical, industrial, and governmental people in Europe the advantages of NTSC, RCA had already spent $500,000 on the development of a mobile unit completely equipped and ready to operate on the European 50-cycle power 'supply and 625-lines standard. RCA had overcome European objections to NTSC; one variant of the system was compatible with American standards, and other variants of the system would operate on the European power and line standards.

To show that the NTSC system would function on the different European standards, RCA was prepared to spend an additional $250,000 to promote NTSC in Europe. This was tangible evidence of RCA's belief in the importance of the promotion of the NTSC system for the European standard. RCA perceived that the decision on standards made at the C.C.I.R. had far-reaching consequences in determining the standards that would be adopted for color television in European and non-European countries. In his letter, Odorizzi noted that African, Middle Eastern, and Southeast Asian countries tended to adhere to television standards existing in Europe, and it was likely that they would adopt whatever standards of color were approved for Europe (U.S. Dept. of Commerce, 1964, p. 3). He warned the Department of Commerce that American manufacturers would be losing a huge market, if the NTSC system was not adopted as the European standard:

> If the decision goes against the NTSC standards, and in favor of the French SECAM system, the consequent loss to American manufacturers in the sale of equipment, components, license revenue and technical aid—not to mention American technological prestige— will be enormous. Certainly the monetary loss to the United States over the next decade, could be counted in tens of millions, and perhaps hundreds of millions, of dollars. (U.S. Dept. of Commerce, 1964, p. 5)

Most significantly, Odorizzi stated:

> Conversely, the United States' loss would represent an equivalent gain to the French industry, justifying the apparent support being given the SECAM campaign by the French Government. (U.S. Dept. of Commerce, 1964, p. 5)

RCA identified Russia as holding the key vote, as being the pivotal force and country to convince:

> In the final analysis, the votes of the Soviet Union and its satellites will be extremely influential, if not controlling, in deciding the color television standards to be adopted for Europe. (U.S. Dept. of Commerce, 1964, p. 3)

Although RCA recognized how important the votes of the Soviet Union and eastern European Communist countries were to NTSC's chances of becoming the European standard, promotional efforts for NTSC in these countries were hampered by security barriers (Houser & Frahm, 1974; McQuade, 1971; Warnke & Morris, 1969). RCA had difficulty in obtaining Commerce Department permission to export a completely equipped, mobile demonstration unit to the Soviet Union. According to documents declassified by the U.S. government, the video tape recorder, and in particular, its rotating head, were not permitted export. The rotating head had "an extremely critical use in electronic intercept applications by U.S. Defense Agencies." It was expected that if the VTRs were exported to these countries, "they would find parallel applications" (U.S. Dept. of Commerce, 1964).

While the U.S.S.R. was known to have produced a few television tape recorders, U.S. equipment was considered to be superior and to contain advanced technology and circuitry which eastern European countries had not been able to duplicate. Two of the significant components were the high-quality rotary quadruplex recording heads and the electronically variable delay lines. Although the Soviets did have rotary heads, they were supposedly inferior products.

The Defense Department claimed to have invested over $10 million (a later estimate was $26 million) over five years, "to advance the rotary head recording to state-of-the-art, beyond the initial TV recording stage," to permit use of this technique for classified purposes (Memorandum of November 17, 1964). This support made major contributions to the techniques of color TV recording.

The so-called TR-4 equipment was known to contain practically all of the techniques that had critical value to defense applications. These included suppression of the head-switching transients to levels below slot noise, basic improvements in electromechanical servo-systems necessary to permit electronic flutter correction, dynamically servoed electronically variable delay lines for flutter and time-base correction, and linearized electronics that reduce spurious products to 35 decibels below signal levels (earlier TV recorders evidently often produced spurious products exceeding signal levels which could not be tolerated for strategic applications) (U.S. Dept. of Commerce, 1964, Attachment 2, pp. 1-2).

RCA sought to combat French propaganda, namely, that a tape recorder could not be utilized with the U.S. system. The French had claimed this was a disadvantage of the American system and proved it by demonstrating how the system would not work with an old tape recorder. RCA was particularly anxious to send the new recorder abroad in order to demonstrate that it did furnish an excellent picture (U.S. Dept. of Commerce, 1964, Minutes 45, p. 19). Hence, it was extremely important for RCA to export the video tape recorder for the foreign transmissions and demonstrations.

Program recording is an important and integral function of all broadcasting, and programs not taped and edited in advance are seldom transmitted. How could the Russians be expected to back and adopt a system whose parts might very well be inoperable, incomplete, or unobtainable? The documents declassified by the U.S. government which contain all the minutes of the debates on this issue in the Advisory Committee on Export Policy Structure (A.C.E.P.) do not discuss this question. (See Dept. of State Telegram 1741; Dept. of State Telegram 222; Letters from RCA 12/17/64, 12/18/64; Memorandum 11/30/64; Memorandum 12/22/64; Memorandum 3/12/65; Memorandum 3/22/65; Memorandum undated, Memorandum—Briefing)

American attention was focused instead on identifying the sources of national security risk arising from the release of the VTRs. This was not a facile task, because there was unreliable information concerning the potential sources of risk. For example, the extent of prior access and retail availability of the recorders to the Soviet Union and public in general was not known. Neither was there any precise information regarding how many recorders were at large (at least two VTRs of the model under consideration had already been sent to Japan and England), or whether the Russians had already examined or obtained these VTRs. (U.S. Dept. of Commerce, 1964, Minutes 49). It was possibly already "too late to worry about the loss of technology," if the Soviet Union had "ready access" to the recorders in the United States where they were relatively inexpensive—about $60,000—and easily available. It was doubtful whether any of the recorder technology was not already known to the Russians (U.S. Dept. of Commerce, 1964, Minutes 49, p. 24). Indeed, there were reports of the unguarded exhibit of these same recorders at a U.S.I.A. show in the Soviet Union in 1964.[10]

Yet, the Defense Department representative opposed permitting RCA to demonstrate NTSC with the recorder, and recommended to the O.C. that the U.S. system should only be "demonstrated by use of a camera" (U.S. Dept. of Commerce, 1964, Minutes 45, p. 21). While this was technically feasible, such a demonstration would in no way have counteracted the damaging French propaganda concerning the system's performance with a VTR, nor offered proof of this to the Russians. The main purpose of the demonstration was to prove that a tape recorder could be used with the U.S. system. For RCA to demonstrate the system without a recorder would not have accomplished anything constructive in favor of the NTSC system.

The opinions of the other O.C. members (representatives from the Departments of State, Commerce, N.A.S.A., and C.I.A.) were divided between favoring the RCA transaction for foreign policy and commercial reasons, and opposing it on security grounds. It was eventually decided that if the equipment were displayed in Moscow under effective safeguards, the risk of losing the technology by mere visual inspection would be "virtually zero" (U.S. Dept. of Commerce, 1964, Minutes 49, p. 3).

RCA was finally permitted to display the VTRs in Russia under strict security measures. However, the company was not permitted to agree to the sale, rental, lease, gift, or other disposition of the tape recorder in eastern Europe. Nor were these countries allowed at the time to test or experiment with it.

Until shortly before the C.C.I.R. meeting in Vienna to determine the European color television standard, the American government did not have a clear perspective on the political and economic stakes involved. The A.C.E.P. committee was still debating the significance of the views of eastern European Communist countries, in light of their lower living standards and the likelihood of their moving less quickly to the utilization of color television than western European countries (U.S. Dept. of Commerce, 1964, Minutes 5, p. 6).

In fact, the Soviet Union was prepared to install a color television system. The votes of eastern European countries were important as a pivotal force to sway the votes of uncommitted and Third-World nations. The French understood their importance and had been work-

---

[10]Dr. George Brown of RCA Labs related to the author his experiences of handling unguarded identical recorders in the U.S.I.A. Russian exhibit. Dr. Brown examined these recorders, noting their serial and type numbers, and nobody prevented him from doing so. Furthermore, these recorder developments had all been carefully noted by engineers in various technical journals, available to anyone.

ing hard for months to obtain them. By contrast, in the United States, the Russians were suspected of "using the C.C.I.R. as a device to obtain the equipment for other purposes than TV" (U.S. Dept. of Commerce, 1964, Minutes 5, p. 7). The declassified documents reveal that O.C. members were convinced that the Russians would be so delighted at the prospect of getting the American technology, that no efforts were needed by the American government to sell the system. The American system would sell itself. From the American perspective, the problem seemed to be how could the United States "prevent the Soviets from becoming so "sold" on the recorder" that they would "insist on having it as the price for their vote on the European System" or would otherwise "make, or consent to its sale or gift an issue of high foreign policy?"[11]

Three weeks later, approximately 21 days before the Vienna conference, the Commerce Interagency Advisory Committee recommendation was suddenly reversed. This change was not precipitated by the realization that the risks to national security were minimal or that the export markets for American-made color television equipment would be lost. Rather, it was an outgrowth of the Defense Department's discovery that the VTR head had not been developed with Defense funds.

From the viewpoint of the Defense Department, there was no longer any material reason to object to the sale and export of the video tape recording head (U.S. Dept. of Commerce, 1964, Minutes 9, p. 23). When attention was drawn to a remark in the A.C.E.P. record that D.O.D. had spent $26,514,277 for wideband rotary-head recorder development and hardware, the Defense representative explained that "the particular head on this particular recorder" was a commercial development. The Defense Department had made modifications in a commercial instrument for Defense uses, and the Department's decision not to oppose the export of the VTR was now "based on the fact that they did not pay for the development of the RCA head" (U.S. Dept. of Commerce, 1964 Minutes 9, p. 23).

The chairman of O.C. reminded the Defense Department representative that the Export Control Act did not "limit control to items built with U.S. money, nor does it limit an agency to providing information and advice only on things it has paid for in advance" (U.S. Dept. of Commerce, 1964 Minutes 9, p. 23).

The elimination of the Defense Department's objection to the export of the VTR, on the grounds that it had not paid for the

---

[11]Memorandum to Thomas G. Wyman, Dec. 22, 1964; edited and declassified document, October 21, 1975.

development of this particular head, occurred just a few weeks prior to the C.C.I.R. convention. By this time the French had almost concluded their negotiations and accord with the Russians. It is possible that the delay caused by the Defense Department's earlier objections to the export of the American VTR may have been partially responsible for the American loss and the French success in gaining this market.

On March 12, 1965, the Commerce Department's top-level interagency advisory group, the cabinet-level Export Control Review Board (E.C.R.B.) including the Secretaries of Commerce (Conner), State (Rusk), Deputy Secretary of Defense (Vance), and Director of the C.I.A. (McCone), reviewed policy suggestions that would support the sale of the U.S. color television system to the U.S.S.R. and other nations. The Board discussed recommendations that: (1) RCA should receive cordially the anticipated visit of a Soviet technical delegation and give it information on the workings and manufacture of color sets and color studio equipment; (2) sanction the sale to the U.S.S.R. of the equipment and technology necessary to support a Soviet color television industry, lest the U.S.S.R. turn to western European sources for that assistance; and (3) instruct American Foreign Service posts to assist actively and support U.S. industry representatives in selling the U.S. color television system (U.S. Export Control Review Board, 1965).

This time the requests were neither approved or denied: action was delayed. With E.C.R.B. concurrence, Secretary Conner recommended that they should be "conditioned on RCA's obtaining a favorable answer from the U.S.S.R. regarding support for Europe's adoption of the NTSC system" (U.S. Export Control Review Board, 1965). RCA was to be informed that

> the U.S. was not willing to license actual exports of any of the NTSC system to the U.S.S.R. or any Bloc country at this time, and that RCA officials could tell the U.S.S.R. officials that the U.S. would be willing to license the entire NTSC system, including the recorder, as a complete package, if the U.S.S.R. would support and vote for the adoption of the NTSC system by Europe. (U.S. Export Control Review Board, 1965).

In essence, Secretary Conner had recommended that RCA be allowed to sell the system as a whole (and not the tape recorder or any other components alone), *conditioned* on RCA getting assurances from the Soviets that they would vote and work for the adoption of the U.S. standards at the March meeting of the C.C.I.R. in Vienna (Memorandum of Conference, 1965).

The decision to sell the RCA system as a whole and not piece-meal was commercially logical in view of the COCOM restrictions on the tape recorder.[12] If the color TV tape recorder or any other COCOM embargo item were to be exported to the Soviet Union or eastern European Communist nations, a special exception would have to be obtained and agreed to unanimously by all the COCOM countries. If the recorder were merely part of a complete system which was not on the COCOM embargo list, under a COCOM administrative principle it would then be possible for the United States to approve the license without having to obtain unanimous COCOM approval and as a result, run the risk of a French veto (Memorandum of Conference, 1965). Thus, U.S. government officials had decided to approve a sale of RCA's complete NTSC system, including the recorder, but not a sale of the recorder or any other COCOM component alone.

The ability of RCA to promote the American system in the U.S.S.R. had been constrained by A.C.E.P., E.C.R.B., and COCOM-related restrictions. The company regarded the latest decision from E.C.R.B. favorably. This strategy avoided the possibility of the French veto. The president of RCA claimed "the Secretary's decision to deal only with a sale of the whole RCA system, and to put it on a conditional basis to the Soviets, was a good thing," from the standpoint of his company, because it "would enable RCA and the U.S. to have a better bargaining position with the Soviets" (Memorandum of Conference, 1965).

The extent to which furnishing technology to the Soviets to make components of a color TV system would pose a competitive threat to RCA and other U.S. firms was discussed by RCA officials and the director of the Commerce Department Office of Export Control. RCA executives maintained that they had no concern about the Soviets being able to do this for years, since they would have problems without RCA's help. It was noted that, notwithstanding any claims the French were making to the Soviets regarding the availability of a complete French system including tape recorder and technology, the French were just as bound by COCOM rules as the U.S., both with respect to the requirements for exceptions of particular strategic items and the availability of the administrative principle,

---

[12] COCOM is the acronym for "Coordinating Committee". It was "established circa 1950 for the purpose of controlling directly or indirectly shipments of strategic goods and technology to the U.S.S.R. and Eastern Europe. Its members included Japan and all N.A.T.O. countries except Iceland" (Interview with Mr. Theodore Thau, executive secretary of the E.C.R.B. and A.C.E.P., and chairman, O.C., 1961-72, in Summer, 1977).

in the event that a complete system should be offered. However, it was also remarked that unlike the American system, the French system did not utilize separate tape recorders (Memorandum of Conference, 1965).

Six days before the Vienna conference, Secretary Rusk wired the embassies in Moscow, London, Paris, and Vienna that the ambassador to the U.S.S.R. was authorized to advise Rudnev or other appropriate Soviet officials that the U.S. government was prepared to authorize export to the U.S.S.R. of the entire NTSC color television system including all components, contingent upon Soviet support of the NTSC system. The ambassador was instructed to

> emphasize that [the] decision was taken after due consideration at highest levels [of the] U.S.G. (U.S. government) and represents strong support of the U.S.G. for worldwide adoption [of the] NTSC color television system. It further [was] indicative of steps U.S.G. [was] taking to improve trade relations with (the) U.S.S.R.[13]

So, in 1965 the U.S. government finally arrived at the same conclusion reached by the French government a few years earlier: to court the Soviets. While the success of the French strategy to win the support of the Soviet Union was due in part to French efforts and the Soviet predisposition to accept favorable French terms, the success of the French strategy happened also because the Americans did not seize the initiative sooner. RCA's attempts to promote the American system in the Soviet Union encountered problems over the export of the VTR component. When the American government determined that the VTR could be exported, American efforts to win the support of the Soviet Union were too late. Had the permission for the export of the VTR been granted much sooner, it is possible that the French may not have created their export market with the help of the Soviet Union.

---

[13] Department of state telegram to the American Embassy, Moscow 2486, March 17, 1965. (Edited and declassified document, October 21, 1975.)

5
SECAM:
French Ambitions
and International Outcome

INTRODUCTION

The French government's approach to developing a color television industry in France had two foci: internally, to marshall domestic support behind the development of industrial manufacturing for SECAM and externally, to create and expand a market for the products. From their experience in attempting to build an indigenous capability in the computer industry ("L'Affaire Bull"), the French had learned that certain elements were crucial to the successful development of an independent electronics industry. Foremost among the internal conditions was the ownership of French technology patents, the industrial potential to manufacture them, and market protection to allow their development. The SECAM patent for color television provided the French with their own technology and the opportunity to fulfill these criteria.

The first step in this direction was the unification of the television industry behind the same goal, support for SECAM. This was a complicated project requiring skillful negotiations to placate the jealousy and distrust levied against CSF-CFT in the industry. The confidence of French manufacturers had to be gained on both the economic and technical levels. The manufacturers needed to be reassured that support for SECAM would not raise industrial costs for them, be more expensive to manufacture, or entail higher royalty fees than NTSC. On technical grounds, NTSC was already a proven system, while SECAM was still a relatively unknown product. The technical and manufacturing problems of SECAM had not yet been fully explored; American manufacturers had experienced and solved NTSC production problems.

The government intervened to allay these apprehensions. Tension was reduced by setting royalty fees at a low price for domestic manufacturers. Arrangements were made for companies to conduct technical tests on SECAM to alleviate misgivings about its operation and production. Firms were patriotically encouraged to consider the prestige of France, of having a domestic (rather than an individual company's) technology adopted as the standard for Europe, and the export benefits this would bring for the entire French industry.

The next step in the government's approach to creating a color television industry was the promotion of SECAM abroad for the European standard. The creation of this external market for SECAM was contingent upon domestic support not only from the television industry, but from all government agencies. This posed a problem for members of the O.R.T.F., the government's technical broadcasting organization, which resented the intrusion of politics into its realm of technical expertise. Hostility toward SECAM was further exacerbated by the circumstance that SECAM's inventor, Henri de France, was not affiliated with O.R.T.F. (See Chapter 2, footnote 1, p. 13.) Although the official government directive to promulgate SECAM did not have O.R.T.F.'s complete patronage, O.R.T.F. bureaucrats did not have the independence or freedom to ignore it. The expression of their dissatisfaction was evident at the C.C.I.R. meeting in Vienna in 1965.

VIENNA, 1965

On March 22, 1965, a joint communiqué was issued by Alain Peyrefitte, minister of information in France, and Sergei Vinogradov, Soviet ambassador to France, in which France and the Soviet Union agreed to cooperate on the adoption of a color television system based on the SECAM standard (Accord entre le gouvernement de la République Francaise, 1965). While American authorities delayed permission for the export of the NTSC system and all its components to the Soviet Union, French officials had been concluding a Franco-Soviet accord.

The accord was greeted in the French press as a great victory for the technical genius of the country and as an American defeat (Galuce, 1965; Soviet endorses French color TV, 1965). The French minister of information hailed the occasion as a "glorious day for the human race" (May, 1965; Mooney, 1965). But the Franco-Soviet agreement was not received with such enthusiasm world-wide. In particular, the agreement and the timing of its announcement generated deep tensions and hostility among C.C.I.R. delegates, including some of the French.[14]

Most of the Western representatives were said to be very unhappy about this kind of politicking and feared that if nations tried to force decisions by such methods, it could well cause a breakup of the C.C.I.R. (TV conference splits over color system, 1965). Western European delegations to the C.C.I.R. resented the manner in which France had courted Soviet support for SECAM.[15] Coming as it did, prior to the Vienna discussions, the announcement of the accord was interpreted as a rebuff to the C.C.I.R. itself. In effect, France and the Soviet Union had proclaimed intentions of proceeding with SECAM, regardless of the C.C.I.R. decision. For years, technical members of the C.C.I.R. had labored to control the proliferation of multiple television standards and to unify Europe with one color television system. Now, regardless of the system chosen by the delegates, the world would have at least two, and perhaps even three, systems. All that costly effort was viewed as fruitless by the task-force members of the C.C.I.R. As one delegation chief asked,

> Why announce it just now? They [the French and the Soviets] are both here. Why could they not wait until the conference has gone over the pros and cons, the pluses and minuses in each system, in order to secure the generally accepted best for a European solution? (Bourne, 1965).

The timing of the announcement signified that the politicians had determined the course of events and not the technical experts who had gathered in Vienna. The technical representatives bitterly resented the intervention and authority of politicians in their domain. The decision on color television systems represented the first time politicians instead of technical experts headed delegations to the C.C.I.R. (See also Le Général de Gaulle, 1965; Lavallard, 1965; Vichney, 1965a).

---

[14]See the following for Franco-American interpretations of the Franco-Soviet Accord: De Montalais (1965); Escarpit (1965); Fauques (1965); Galuce (1965); L'industrie électronique (1966); Mallein (1965b); News briefs (1965); Soviet endorses French color TV (1965); L'U.R.S.S. choisit le procédé Francais (1965); Vichney (1965d).

[15]See also Business international: Colour TV—each to his own (1965); Business international: You, too, can QAM (1965); Meeting fails to set color TV standards (1965); Russia joins France (1965).

The friction between the two groups was particularly rife among the French delegates. Although the French had publicly committed their delegation to the SECAM system, not all members of the delegation agreed. The technical representatives from O.R.T.F. had fought for European technical unity and were willing to back PAL if necessary to obtain it. While they did not support the advance announcement of the Franco-Soviet accord, they were powerless to oppose it. As a result, this group elicited sympathy from their counterparts on other delegations, who felt that there was no need to force politics into the decision (Bourne, 1965). Had the technicians been left alone, some French technical experts believe, a unified decision backing SECAM might have been reached. As it was, many technical representatives from western European nations deplored the French government for its heavy-handedness, independence, and disregard for the operation of the C.C.I.R.

From the French political perspective, the timing of the announcement fulfilled its objectives. French ambitions had originally focused on making SECAM the European color television standard. The development of the German PAL system had weakened French chances for this position. The French confronted the possibility that SECAM would have no external market, unless France could convince uncommitted, Third World, and French-speaking countries to support SECAM. In order to swing votes from these countries, the French had to demonstrate that their system was a realistic contender against the American and German competition. In this respect, the Russian backing achieved its designed effect. Had the French announced the agreement after the meeting was underway or over, the psychological and political impact would have been diminished; and, top French government officials believe, they would have lost much of their eventual support.

The Americans and Germans responded to pressures from the Franco-Soviet coupling by merging NTSC and PAL into a single unit known as QUAM (for Quadrature Amplitude Modulation), or as the French mockingly called the hurried American-German action, "Quick Austrian Mixture" (TV conference splits over color television systems, 1965; see also Bonn and U.S. reach accord, 1965; Mallein, 1965a, pp. 15-16; U.S. Bonn agree to merge, 1965; U.S. Bonn color TV system is Europe's 2nd, 1965; U.S., West Germany adopt compromise plan, 1965; Vienna color TV parley, 1965). QUAM was a concept, not a totally new system. It combined the similar elements of the NTSC and PAL systems and thus distinguished them from SECAM. Its purpose was to unite the remaining votes so that the delegates would vote for one system rather than two systems. Splitting the votes between NTSC and PAL would have weakened the opposition to SECAM. When the delegates voted for QUAM, it did not mean they would install QUAM in their countries. Rather, they would install either the NTSC or PAL systems, whichever they preferred. QUAM merely indicated that the delegates wanted an alternative to the SECAM system. It seems that the concept of QUAM was not entirely clear to the delegates until after the conference ended. Early news releases implied that the general idea of QUAM was more in the nature of a fourth television system. Following the termination of the conference, spokesmen for the PAL-NTSC forces clarified that the two systems would not be merged in actuality:

> The decision to coin the name QUAM was a tactical measure to avoid splitting up our forces, not the creation of a new technical system. (Vienna color TV parley, 1965)

The final vote at the 1965 conference in Vienna did not decide which system Europe would adopt. The meeting ended in an impasse in the form of a two-way split: France's SECAM received 21 votes; QUAM received 18. Included in the French votes were the anticipated Communist-bloc countries and four African nations, former French colonies lacking black-and-white television services (Vienna color TV parley, 1965; see also Delacour, 1965; Vichney, 1965b, 1965c).

In general, voting in the C.C.I.R. followed traditional patterns of linkage and conflict where the voters themselves had no color television system to export or promote. The determination of which color television system countries favored, was based to a large measure on whether nations shared old colonial ties, linguistic and cultural unity, or similar political philosophies with one of the countries promoting a system. Russia was able to carry the eastern European Communist countries in the vote for SECAM, while France was able to swing the support of African, Francophone countries. Northern European, Scandanavian countries followed Germany. The Dutch supported NTSC until it appeared to lose all chance for the European standard, and then switched to support PAL. (The Dutch had been interested in economies of scale possible in producing for one color television standard. If Europe was split on color television systems, the Dutch still were assured a strong market position through their company, Radiotechnique, manufacturing for SECAM in France, and Philips manufacturing for PAL and the rest of Europe (Philips fabriquera les trois, 1968). Britain and Australia followed the pattern established by the United States and Germany.

Those nations voting for the United States-German systems coalition included most of the western European countries prepared to initiate one system or another. Interpreting the votes in terms of quantity might lead to the supposition that France was the "victor," as Paris newspaper hastily headlined the event. If the votes are judged on the criterion of preparedness to install a color television system, the interpretation is different. Only the Soviet Union (among the French supporters) was in a position to begin immediate work on a color television system.

The adjournment of the meeting was marked with a communiqué promising to resume consideration of the matter in Oslo in 1966, because all participants were concerned that efforts to secure agreement on a single system should continue.

OSLO, 1966

The C.C.I.R. XIth Plenary Assembly resumed its discussions of a color television standard for Europe in Oslo in 1966. It ended without an agreement on a single system for 625-line color television, as it had done in Vienna in 1965 (Hansen, 1966, p. 138). At the Oslo conference, 15 delegates voted for SECAM IIIb, a later French development of SECAM; twelve delegates opted for PAL; six delegates abstained or had no preference, while three delegations voted for SECAM IV (Hansen, 1966, p. 138; see also From Russia with love, 1966; Gould, 1966).

SECAM IV was a Russian system (sometimes referred to as N.I.R.) which had been perfected after the Russians had agreed in the March 1965 communiqué to adopt the French SECAM system. Other than its name, it had little in common with the French system. Its fundamental principles of operation were closer in technology to the PAL and NTSC systems; it could be linked to them with little difficulty. Because it bore the French name SECAM and yet was compatible with the other systems, some of the delegates thought SECAM IV would be an excellent compromise choice. It was not selected at Oslo, primarily because it had not been fully tested; it was still in the laboratory stages. Most countries in western Europe were anxious to proceed with color television immediately and did not want to wait for SECAM IV to pass the necessary testing. There were some rumors that France was not favorable toward SECAM IV because it was not possible on such a short basis to determine exactly how much of the revenue from the patents would belong to whom (Political hues, 1966; see also Business international: All PALS TOGETHER, 1966; Halberstrom, 1966).

In an attempt to achieve unanimity, the Danish delegation pointed out that PAL could be "regarded as much a development of the SECAM system as of the NTSC," and was, therefore, "a truly international system." Like SECAM, it involved a line-by-line switching process and a delay-line store in the receivers; but, it was also a QUAM system—the modulation feature of NTSC. The Danes suggested that PAL should be renamed SEQUAM (Sequential European Quadrature Amplitude Memory method). While many delegations (including the Germans) supported this effort to avoid the drift to two European systems, the Franco-Soviet coalition did not (Political hues, 1966; see also Business international: All PALS TOGETHER, 1966). Thus, the Oslo meeting ended in the same way as the Vienna meeting; the world now was divided by three color television systems.

Although the French had not fulfilled part of their original objective to make SECAM the European standard for color television systems, they had managed to create a market for SECAM as the standard for Third World and eastern European Communist nations. This external market for SECAM did not offer the possibility of immediate and profitable returns on the financial investment in SECAM. While it was not on the scale or as lucrative as they had planned at the outset, it did provide a future outlet for French SECAM products when the domestic market became saturated.

The French believed that the differences in standards would prevent large western European consumer electronics firms from exporting into France, because the market would be too limited to permit effective economies of scale in production. The French expected that the differences in standards would protect their color television industry during its developmental stages, until it was strong enough to compete.

With the development of the PAL system, the French had almost lost the possibility of finding an external market for SECAM. The outcome of the C.C.I.R. conference in Oslo was to provide the French with a market for SECAM, the possibility to recoup financial investments in the technology through patent royalty rights, and the guarantee that France would not be isolated in the world by a unique color television standard (as it had been by the monochrome lines standard).

SECAM, 1978: A PERSPECTIVE
OF TWELVE YEARS

The French government guaranteed the original adoption of SECAM outside France through its alliance with Russia. For more than a decade it has maintained and expanded the horizons for SECAM by initiating impressive sales orders and by opening up new markets abroad for SECAM on a continuing basis.[16] The sales have been boosted by the display of political importance the French government has attached to the adoption of its color television system technology. This is evident in the inclusion of SECAM in discussions at international meetings at the prime ministerial level; in the portrayal of SECAM's adoption by another country as the "bonne geste" of that nation toward France; in the consideration of SECAM as part of other large-scale technical trade negotiations; and in the linking of certain sales of other technologies to its adoption (Calabuig, 1974; Kilborn, 1966).

The French government has encouraged SECAM color television sales by assuming responsibility for marketing it. Through the establishment of highly coordinated organizations in the government itself, the state is involved in assisting with the sales of SECAM from beginning to end. In France the government performs many of the tasks fulfilled by private companies in other nations. It is the French government which arranges for assistance in marketing surveys and research, political entree, promotional tours, exhibitions, fairs, demonstrations, technical training, technical aid, financial aid, credit, etc.

The attitude of the French government with regard to SECAM is that potential buyers must be assiduously courted. An elaborate structure exists within the government and in private industry to achieve the successful completion of this objective. Five government agencies are directly involved in this effort, as well as a few privately run, government-affiliated organizations. The effort is centralized and coordinated through the Délégation Interministérielle de la Télévision en Couleurs (D.I.Tv.C.), located in La Direction des Industries Électroniques et de l'Informatique in the Ministère de l'Industrie et de la Recherche (M.I.R.). Offices handling color television promotion are also found in the Ministère de l'Information,

---

[16]The French efforts to sell SECAM and SECAM products have continued worldwide. See Accord Franco-Egyptien (1972); Arabie Saudite (1972); Arnaud (1970); La bataille de la télé (1971); Business international: Europe's Mare Nostrum (1972); Carenzo (1975); De Latil (1967, 1974, b,c,d); Electronics abroad: Argentina (1965); Electronics abroad: Argentina—bridgehead for SECAM (1965); Electronics abroad: Austria (1975); Electronics abroad: France—African campaign (1966); Electronics abroad: India—market for Red TV (1965); Electronics abroad: Latin America—dumping PAL (1968); Electronics abroad: Rumania (1965); Electronics international: Sweden (1969); Le gouvernement Grec (1969); La Hongrie (1969); International report (1975); Jublin (1974); Lachenbruch (1966); La Libye (1971); Newsletter from abroad: Spain (1966); Nyehan (1967, 1968); Peyrefitte a entretenu (1976); Picapier (1969); Le SECAM en Afrique (1971); Tchécoslovaquie (1967); Vichney (1968).

the Ministère des Affaires Étrangères, the Ministère de Finance, and the Ministère de Commerce Extérieure.

The M.I.R., which is concerned with industrial research and development, is responsible for assuring coordination of policy recommendations and compliance in the promotion of SECAM. It appears that the Ministry of Foreign Affairs directs the political and cultural contacts important to SECAM's promotion; the Ministry of Finance determines the taxes and interest on credit and loans extended to buyers of the system, including the feasibility of making them, (in conjunction with COFACE, Compagnie Francaise pour l'Assurance de la Commerce Extérieure, an import-export insurance-type of operation); the Ministry of International Commerce determines the market situation and business conditions existing in different countries and sponsors market research to ascertain whether and why SECAM would sell there; and the Ministry of Information serves as a clearing house for public announcements and information about the government's promotional endeavors of SECAM.

The two organizations wielding the most clout in promoting and selling SECAM are (privately run, although government-sponsored groups) INTERSECAM and SOFRATEV. INTERSECAM was formed in March, 1968, under the joint aegis of the O.R.T.F., F.N.I.E., and C.F.T. as a nonprofit organization ("à but non lucratif") with the charter of "la défense, la promotion et la diffusion à l'étranger, par tous les moyens appropriés, de procédé SECAM de télévision couleur" (Dibie 1972; Temple, 1968). INTERSECAM's mission was to use every appropriate means to promote, defend, and diffuse the SECAM color television system abroad. For this purpose, INTERSECAM receives funding from two main sources, the founding organizations and the government. The founding organizations contribute to an annual budget which covers the general costs of operations. For specific promotional efforts, the state pays the bill. Financing for this, "les actions particulières de promotion," is approved by the D.I.Tv.C. (Dibie, undated).

SOFRATEV (Société Francaise d'Études et de Réalisations d'Équipements de Radiodiffusion et la de Télévision) was created in July, 1973, with a capital base of one million francs (approximately $225,000-$250,000). Fifty-one percent of that money was committed by O.R.T.F. through an organization called Public de Diffusion, which was established to handle O.R.T.F. transactions following a reorganization plan scheduled to take effect in January, 1975. The remainder (49 percent), came from 11 banks, each committing about 4.45 percent. SOFRATEV works in conjunction with INTER-

SECAM. While INTERSECAM promotes SECAM, SOFRATEV conducts all studies on technical or financial problems relative to radio, television, and all other audiovisual technologies abroad. SOFRATEV's charter comprises (but does not deal exclusively with) SECAM, as does the INTERSECAM organization (Tessier, 1975).

In the first eighteen months of operation, SOFRATEV conducted studies on the construction of a radio-television broadcasting building in Tripoli, Libya; considered the possibilities of creating a center for a national cinema also in Tripoli; did preliminary work on a center to produce television programs in Tunisia; carried out preliminary investigations for a radio-television broadcasting building in Morocco; supervised equipment for "La Cité d'Information" in Zaire; and examined radio coverage in Peru. SOFRATEV also worked on the establishment of a color television network in Saudi Arabia via the creation of an international subsidiary, L'Adete, in which SOFRATEV is the majority stockholder. In Iran, SOFRATEV counselled Iranian television engineers on the switch to color and founded a Franco-Iranian engineering institute in Teheran to conduct research on SECAM (Tessier, 1975).

SOFRATEV's accomplishments in Saudi Arabia and Iran are typical of the kind of technical cooperation the French hoped to establish with SECAM. Eventually, they aspire for SOFRATEV to assume the responsibility for all the technical promotion, not only of SECAM but of other French telecommunications technologies. Toward this objective, SOFRATEV intervenes to assist in the majority of countries adopting SECAM for the purpose of furnishing the means and expertise to install the equipment and necessary engineering from beginning to end. Without these technical efforts, French government officials believe, the politics and promotion of SECAM would have had little consequence or benefit for the French economy.

INTERSECAM and SOFRATEV coordinate their efforts to promote SECAM abroad. Generally, INTERSECAM establishes the political, cultural, and financial support to initiate a tour or demonstration of SECAM. SOFRATEV handles the technical operation, preparations, and actual demonstrations of the system. These tours are often selected to coincide with an important telespectacular event, such as the Olympic games, where the size of the audience watching color television is guaranteed to be large. In this way, the French assure themselves of the most dramatic impact on the largest number of people. The goodwill generated by the impression of the event motivates host countries to favor SECAM. This technique has been employed by all the competing systems to some degree.

Special demonstrations of SECAM are also conducted in France for visiting dignitaries. Afterward, these officials are given tours of a special school constructed in 1972 at Bry-sûr-Marne, where everything anybody needs to know about color television is taught. Technicians learn to handle cameras, film, lights, makeup, sound and audio equipment, etc. The French claim that those countries which adopt SECAM may be assured of a fully trained, technical staff to operate and maintain the system in their home countries after this training.

In countries with a high percentage of unskilled personnel, such as those in which SECAM sells well, this is an attractive option. French government officials have indicated that they believe that the school is frequently the decisive factor in a country's acceptance of SECAM. Not only does the country acquire a color television system, it also has the opportunity to upgrade the skills of its labor force. Furthermore, the trained technicians allow the country to be independent of France for the maintenance of the system, should the relationship between the two countries deteriorate. This school is an example of the French government's ability to tailor the sales of its color television system to the needs of its particular market. Whether or not the foreign government purchasing SECAM pays for the training of technicians varies: Iraqis paid their own way; poorer African nations had their technicians trained, courtesy of the French.

Details of the sales orders and technical arrangements are conducted through company channels and the company which has benefited the most from the sales is Thomson-Brandt, a large consumer and professional electronics firm. CSF no longer exists as a manufacturing company. It merged with Thomson; but the royalties for SECAM belong to CFT. CFT is now a patent-holding, royalty-collecting organization for the SECAM patent.

Since the decision to adopt a color television standard is ultimately a governmental (rather than industrial) decision, the French government has been the driving force in selling the SECAM system to other governments (Les Egyptiens se prononcent, 1969; see also Arabie Saudite, 1974; Le Liban, 1969; M. Jobert en Espagne, 1973; Proche-Orient, 1973; Schwoebel, 1973; La visite du Chah d'Iran, 1974). The marketing has been concentrated on a government-to-government level from the earliest stages, which meant that discussions of SECAM were included in almost every high-level, international, governmental negotiation. The French incorporated deals on SECAM as part of diverse trade pacts, scientific exchanges, defense sales, and so on. Agreements concerning the purchase of French "Mirage" jets, defense weaponry, satellite technology, etc., often added some arrangement about adopting SECAM, SECAM equipment, plant installation, or the like, as conditions (tacit or overt) of the sale. SECAM became the gesture of good faith between the two countries. It was a way for another nation to cement its relationship with France, a way of showing appreciation for other favors, assistance, etc.

Two countries, among others, where the French employed the marketing strategy of "la bonne geste" are Iraq and Iran. During a visit by French Prime Minister Chirac to Iraq in December, 1974, newspapers recorded that the two countries had negotiated contracts worth 15 billion francs. Included in the Iraqi commissions were: the construction of a petro-chemical complex and an aluminum factory; the building of a 600-bed military hospital; cooperation in computers and telecommunications equipment; and the adoption of SECAM. Iraq strongly favored the installation of PAL, but according to the French, had wanted to make a "present" to their guest by adopting SECAM:

> Sur l' adoption par l' Irak du procédé SECAM de télévision en couleurs—on rapporte dans les milieux francaise que l' Irak était déjà fortement orienté vers le système concurrent PAL, mais que M. Saddat Hussein a tenu à faire ce "cadeau" à son hôte. (Tatu, 1974a, 1974b)

A few weeks later, Monsieur Chirac accomplished similar results in Iran. When the contracts were signed, the Iranian orders were estimated to be worth 35 billion francs. The benefits were not confined to one industry but involved diverse requests. Among these were: the establishment of five nuclear centers, plus the uranium enrichment necessary for them; the construction of a railroad; the electrification of Iranian railroads; the installation of 500,000 telephone lines; and the sale of arms, agricultural products, and color television. More than any of the other agreements, SECAM was the symbol of the new trade relationship. Newspapers proclaimed that "la volonté de coopération franco-iranienne se manifeste par l' adoption du procédé SECAM" (Passeron, 1974a, 1974b, 1974c).

The French were particularly delighted over the Iranian decision to choose SECAM, because PAL was known to be favored there. "Tout Téhéran estimait, peu avant, que le procédé allemand PAL avait des chances beaucoup plus grandes de l' emporter" (Passeron, 1974b). The Shah was informed that the French president attached "une particulière valeur au choix de SECAM" (Passeron, 1974b; see also Tandis que l' Iran, 1974). The Iranian adoption of SECAM was a sign of the special significance which the Iranians attached to their relationship with France. The agreements provided that the French should supply the Iranians with transmitters, technical assistance, technical training, and the construction of television sets.

Color television is a marketable (though perhaps not yet money-making) commodity in underdeveloped countries because it symbolizes modernity and progress. It represents "the good life" of the future brought into today, for the people of developing countries. Although food sources, medicines, energy installations, desalination projects, professional and skilled labor, etc., may be more important to the economic development and welfare of these nations, the adoption of a color television system is a concrete promise of progress from the government leaders of these less-developed countries to their constituencies.

Color television is highly visible, entering into the homes and village centers throughout a country. By providing continual enjoyment and pleasure, it keeps the population entertained and distracted from the daily problems of survival and dissatisfaction. In this way, it is a form of political control. As a technology of political communication, color television can be used to educate, inform, and amuse the population. (Goar Mestre, 1969; Mexicans learn to read, 1965). It gives the broadcasting nation prestige and status akin to the status of having a national airline. A nation that has a color television system can be regarded as a nation keeping pace with progress, even if that progress is illusory.

Although the motivations behind a nation's selection of a particular television system may vary, generally they involve considerations of linkage and conflict. In cases of linkage, countries may choose a color television system out of the desire to forge closer ties (in trade or defense, for example) with one of the three countries identified with color television technology (The United States, France, and Germany), or with one of the countries already associated by color television with them (such as Japan, Russia, and Great Britain). In most nations the telecommunications organization are government-operated, and the decision concerning color television systems is political. Since the adoption of a color television system is the adoption of a standard, the decision to choose one system instead of another represents a long-term commitment to the political linkage because of the "locked-in" feature of standards discussed in Chapter 1.

Countries frequently adopt one system because rival or enemy nations have adopted a different system (Wetz, 1972). This situation is apt to occur in regions where nations have unfriendly border relations and want to curb or control the flow of information penetrating the airwaves. Conflict situations are not restricted to border regions; often a pattern of political conflict is followed through traditional and linkage alliances. For example, Turkey adopted the German system while Greece adopted the French system; Israel adopted PAL while most Arab countries installed SECAM; China is favoring PAL since Russia adopted SECAM; the U.S.A., U.S.S.R., and China may have three different systems; it is possible to describe many similar political patterns of technology adoption in color television systems. Let it suffice to say that it appears that when governments have no similar technology to promote, export, or license, their support for compatible technical standards approximates current political interests and objectives at the national level.[17]

The governments to whom France is marketing SECAM want color television to maintain political control, to buy the dream of progress, to forge closer political ties, or to control information penetrating their airwaves. The question is, how do they afford it? The French have devised a highly flexible monetary arrangement to extend credit and loans for the purchase of SECAM. Some countries receive parts of the system as "gifts" and pay for the rest.

French financial assistance programs and intensive promotional efforts have helped create export markets for French color television products. The most recent statistics from the U.N. *World Trade Annual* (1971, 1972, 1975) reflect the growing success of these efforts: in 1971 the value of color television receivers exported from France was almost $7 million; in 1972 this value was nearly $10 million; by 1975 the export market for French color television sets was valued at nearly $28 million.

There are several other indicators to consider in assessing the value of the French color television industry. Domestic sales of color television sets accounted for approximately $750 million in 1975.[18] Patent rights and royalty fees for SECAM in 1975 were worth about $5 million (Jublin, 1975). The technical assistance and support which the French export to those countries adopting SECAM is estimated to be worth over $100 million. In addition, there are sales of professional equipment for studios, electronic components for the television sets, and other equipment estimated to be worth at least $50 million

[17] For the Italians, the choice of a color television system has been politically very difficult. See Business international: Italian television—awful choice (1975); Business international: Italian television—colour politics (1972); Business international: Italian television—too clever by half (1972); Business international: Italy—PAL has enemies (1971); Color TV choice in Italy (1975); Color TV ruling delayed (1975); International newsletter (1972); Italian experts ask selection of German color TV system (1975); Italie: Les republicans menacent de quitter (1972); Italie: Rendez-vous en Sardaigne (1973); Italie: Rome dément avoir subi des pressions (1972); Paris et Rome (1970); Sole (1975a, 1975b); La télévision en couleurs en Italie (1972); Thélier (1969).

[18] One million sets sold at an average of $750 (Guéry, 1975).

yearly (see Electronics abroad: France, 1968).[19] Finally, the French are said to have exported between 15,000 and 20,000 hours of programs in 1972 (Durieux, 1974; Varis, 1973). The color television industry in France is probably now generating over $1 billion of business yearly.[20]

Color television broadcasting began on a regular basis in France in 1967, but domestic sales of color television receivers were slow for several years. While domestic sales of color television sets were comparably slow for the first eight years following its launching in the United States, the problem was different in France (Castel, 1967). In the United States, color television sales were affected by the poor technical quality of the color reception (for example, sudden shifts from red to green). In France, however, these technical problems had been solved by the time color television broadcasting started. Slow television sales in France were caused by other factors. One of these was the high price of the sets: ordinary receivers cost over $1,000 (see Durieux, 1967; Newsletter from abroad: Color-set prices shaved, 1968; Olmer, 1968).[21] Color television sets needed special components in France to operate on the multiple (lines) standards, so that they could receive broadcasts from the 819-lines black-and-white standard as well as the 625-lines standard for color broadcasts. Although France is gradually phasing out the 819-lines standard, dual standards made the price of sets outrageously high. In 1967 only twelve hours per week were transmitted in color; it was not until 1973 that a third network operating completely in color was established. People were reluctant to buy such expensive items for limited color broadcast enjoyment (Des batailles de prix, 1975).

In 1973, 680,000 color sets were sold in comparison to 1,145,000 black-and-white sets (Des batailles de prix, 1975). The French newspaper, *Les Echos* (Des batailles de prix, 1975), noted that black-and-white sets posed a serious threat to color television, because they cost almost three times less (Des batailles de prix, 1975). In addition to the cost of the set, a 20 percent TVA (added value) tax was levied against the price of a color television (French TV

[19]In 1968 this market was estimated to be worth $30 million for French makers of electronic telecommunications and broadcasting equipment. See also Fight goes worldwide (1964), in which the estimate of the market is $50 million.

[20]This estimate is based on the above information and opinions of marketing specialists in American multinational color television firms. It is a conservative gross estimate.

[21]In 1977 the average cost of a color television set was between $500 and $750. See also Il faut unifier les standards de notre télévision (1967); Lavallard (1973); Lilt (1967); TV la couleur et le noir (1966).

makers, 1970; Taxe spéciale, 1975). Stores reported that more than 50 percent of the demands for credit to buy color televisions were rejected or the terms were made too unfavorable for the buyer (Des batailles de prix, 1975; Laveron, 1975). Furthermore, people were discouraged from purchasing color television sets, because the quality of the programming was poor during the early years.

The French color television industry has only recently started to grow (Fédération Nationale des Industries Électroniques, 1974). In 1967 there was less than one color television per thousand televisions in service; between 1968 and 1969, there were three to nine color sets per thousand televisions. In 1971 1.9 percent of the sets in operation were color, and in 1972 4.7 percent of the sets were color (De Latil, 1974b). By 1974 over 14 percent of television sets in service were color (Guéry, 1974). Yet, in 1974 only 78.5 percent of French households had television sets (De Latil, 1974a). The French domestic market is far from saturated and, with the export market, should provide growth potential for the color television receiver industry in the future.

Did the French succeed in creating a color television industry? Since 1976 the color television industry in France has annually generated over $1 billion of business, representing about 0.5 percent of the French GNP. To put this accomplishment in perspective, there are a limited number of industries in the United States which generate more than 0.5 percent of the American GNP. In commercial terms, the French government's efforts to create an industry can be deemed quite successful.

What has made this success possible? From the outset, industrial, governmental, technical, and political factors have combined to enable the French to fulfill their ambitions to develop a color television industry. These included: French industrial ownership of the patent rights for SECAM and industrial cooperation (from government pressures) to manufacture for the SECAM standard; French governmental ability to alter marketing strategies for SECAM to fit changing political conditions and to organize elaborate programs and structures to promote export sales; the employment of differences in standards to protect French domestic industrial development and to create an export market in less developed, Third World, and French-speaking countries; and political support from Russian and eastern European Communist countries for SECAM in the development of an export market.

The French have been fortunate that many of the Third World nations from the 1960s (Iran, Saudi Arabia, etc.) have developed into oil-rich powers of the 1970s, able to afford the luxury of importing a spectrum of expensive technologies and willing to adopt SECAM as part of the overall negotiations.

The SECAM color television system did not fulfill all French ambitions, for it did not become the European standard. There is a possibility that it could have become the European standard if the Germans had not developed PAL as a response to the French refusal to permit them to manufacture the SECAM patent without charge. The French underestimated German technological ingenuity and lost the lucrative western European market to them. In order to ensure an export market in uncommitted and Third World countries, they made a gift of SECAM to the Russians. This market was far less remunerative than the market the French had aimed to obtain by establishing SECAM as the European standard. The revenues generated by the French color television industry could have been substantially higher if the French had not misjudged the Germans or had been able to exert political influence on technological leadership in Europe.

6
Conclusion

This book has explored the use of technical standards as a non-tariff device for protecting an industry. Many of the same issues arise as in the study of protection by tariffs: Do they work to promote the development of an "infant industry?" Do they raise or lower the productivity of the protected industry? Do they operate in the interest of consumers? Do they restrict international commerce, and if so, what can the international community do about them?

In this case, standards worked as a device for promoting an industry. As one theme of this study illustrated, a state can successfully intervene to support the development of an industry in the private sector. While the success of the development of an industry in the private sector is dependent upon several factors (including industrial capability, technological ownership, economic feasibility, as well as other factors discussed in previous chapters), the ability of a government to exert political control and political influence throughout the process is a key element. In the case of the French color television industry, the government facilitated development from the outset by exercising political control over domestic conflicts of interest, in the electronics industry and in the O.R.T.F., coordinating national resources toward the same goals. One goal was the creation of an export market for color television products, which the French accomplished in part by politically influencing other nations to choose the French color television system (the Franco-Russian accord, the "bonne geste" relationship, etc.).

The results of this study suggest that the chances for a government to succeed in developing an industry in the private sector are increased by limiting opportunities in the development process for factors over which the government has no control or influence. The more control a government exerts over factors related to the production, promotion, sales, and export of a technology, the less likely it is that outside forces can interfere with development plans. A government can minimize intervention opportunities by factors in the development process that cannot be directly controlled (such as regulating the flow of imports by tariffs) by the use of standards.

Second, this research illustrates how standards were employed as nontariff barriers, protecting the French color television industry from German-manufactured color television products. Differences in national technical standards can be effectively utilized to create an industry, but the use of standards as a protective device is limited: a company in one country can always manufacture equipment on the same standard as another company in a foreign country by constructing a plant to manufacture it inside the foreign country (as Radiotechnique did in France). Standards may effectively deter trade, but are not an unsurmountable obstacle.

Differences in standards may also be manipulated by governments to segment markets, thereby creating export possibilities where none existed previously. It is a technique for politically controlling the marketplace by technology. Although differences in standards may have beneficial impacts on the development of an industry, they may simultaneously have negative impacts for communications between countries.

In color television systems, the incompatibility between standards was eventually overcome through technological innovation by transcoding devices. What happens when incompatibility between standards cannot be overcome in communications technologies? As technologies of communication proliferate—in radio, telegraph, telephone, computers, etc.—the problems and consequences of the inability to communicate are severe (even sometimes a matter of survival, such as with microwave landing systems at airports). While international cooperation in telecommunications has been fruitful, it has not always been completely successful, as the case of color television systems illustrates. In establishing national telecommunications standards, it is incumbent upon nations to consider the negative effects which internationally incompatible standards might generate. The increasing complexity of communications technologies and the concommitant growth of areas needing standardization raise serious questions about the process in which international standards are set.

The third theme investigated in this study demonstrates how the present process permits national, political, and economic interests to intervene in international standards decisions, frequently causing countries to opt for incompatibility. As the study of color television systems illustrates, royalties and revenues from patent rights are a major hindrance to international agreements. The search for national political prestige and political objectives also create disunity. No mechanisms in international standards-setting impose agreement. Consequently, international negotiations may breakdown, a circumstance which occurred at the Vienna and Oslo meetings.

International organizations are further hampered in their attempts to establish compatible standards by their dependence on member nations for financial support, technical expertise, and willingness to cooperate. However, if technical decisions are concluded by politicians rather than by technical experts, as they were with color television systems, these organizations may atrophy since they no longer serve a useful purpose. Can mechanisms be developed to ensure their independence and technical freedom to set internationally compatible standards? How can the politics of technology be reduced in international standards negotiations?

A first step might be the internationalization of patents for technologies adopted world-wide. All royalties from the patents would belong to the international organization recommending the standards for the technology. These royalties would cover operating expenses of the international organizations, freeing them in part from contributions of member countries. Each country whose technology contributed some original feature to the standard selected would receive a predetermined percentage of the royalties in return; this would enable the country's industry to recoup financial investments in development.

Since the standard chosen would probably be some combination of the many technologies from different nations, the prestige attached to having a national standard adopted world-wide could be eliminated. The international standard could be renamed after the organization recommending its selection, identified and distinguished by a numerical suffix. For example, the standard for color television systems might not have been cited as the American, German, French, or Russian standards, but as C.C.I.R. Standard Number 1965. This would reduce some of the political problems in establishing an international standard by making the standard itself less nationalistic.

Furthermore, nations could be pressured either to adopt compatible standards for communications technologies, or to install a device enabling communications to take place between incompatible standards. A country would be permitted to retain a standard different from the one internationally recommended, provided that its technology incorporate a mechanism which would guarantee the continual flow of international communications. Perhaps a system of penalties could be enforced against countries refusing to participate. This could be determined by a study on the effectiveness of different penalties utilized internationally against various countries. Penalties might range from international taxes levied on the nonparticipating country to the withholding of key communications materiel imported from participating nations.

Finally, only technical experts who had participated in tests conducted on the different communication systems under consideration would be permitted to negotiate the final agreement and selection of the standard. Politicians would not be accepted as official delegates, and their attendance at these meetings would be prohibited. Political pressure on technical delegates would be reduced by ensuring that the voting results were kept secret and possibly by maintaining no records of an individual delegate's preference.

Why would any nation accept these suggestions for changes in international organizations responsible for setting standards in communications? Primarily because an improvement in the overall process of setting international standards would benefit all nations concerned. An improvement in the system of setting standards would make it more likely that standards would be based on technical criteria. This might eliminate many of the problems generated by competing political and economic interests, apparent in the case of color television systems. Decisions reached in this manner would ensure that international communications would be possible because compatible standards would exist. Furthermore, some economic remuneration would be guaranteed to these nations in which technical contributions had originated, thereby protecting the ability of those industries to recoup financial investments. While recognizing the limitations of these suggestions—including the probability that some nations would never be able to accept them for reasons of national security, competition, hostile relationships, etc.—they are intended as a step toward thinking about changing the international standards-setting process.

International standards-setting in communications technologies could be made more objective, technical, and independent of national interests than currently exists. As long as national, political, and economic interests are permitted to intrude in the decisions, situations of incompatible standards between countries will continue to occur. What is needed in setting a standard is the facility to choose a system which is technically superior, so that technical decisions are based on technical and not other criteria. Attention should be focused on methods to improve *the process* by which standards are set. In the end, the ability of nations to communicate will depend upon that process.

Appendices

A
National and International Organizations

ABU	Asian Broadcasting Union
ACEP	Interagency Advisory Committee on Export Policy
AFNOR	Association Francaise de Normalisation
ANSI	American National Standards Institute
APTU	African Postal and Telecommunications Union
BBC	British Broadcasting Corporation
BSI	British Standards Institution
CCIF	International Telephone Consultative Committee
CCIR	International Radio Consultative Committee
CCIT	International Telegraph Consultative Committee
CCITT	International Telegraph and Telephone Consultative Committee
CECC	The Cenel Electronic Components Committee
CEE	International Commission on Rules for the Approval of Electrical Equipment
CEN	European Committee on the Coordination of Standards
CENEL	European Electrical Standards Coordinating Committee
CENELCOM	European Electrical Standards Coordinating Committee of the Common Market
CENELEC	European Electrical Standards Coordinating Committee
CEPT	Conference of European Postal and Telecommunications Administration
CIA	Central Intelligence Agency
CITEL	Inter-American Telecommunications Conference for Latin America
COFACE	Compagnie Francaise pour l'Assurance de la Commerce Extérieure
COPANT	Pan American Standards Commission
DITvC	Délégation Interministérielle de la Télévision en Couleurs
DNA	Deutscher Normenausschus
DOD	Department of Defense

EBU	European Broadcasting Union
ECRB	Export Control Review Board
EEC	European Economic Community
EFTA	European Free Trade Association
EIA	Electronic Industries Association
FCC	Federal Communications Commission
FNIE	Fédération Nationale des Industries Électroniques
ICAO	International Civil Aviation Organization
IEC	International Electrotechnical Commission
IEEE	Institute of Electrical and Electronics Engineers
IFRB	International Frequency Registration Board
IMCO	Inter-Governmental Maritime Consultative Organization
ISA	International Federation of National Standardizing Associations
ISO	International Organization for Standardization
ITU	International Telecommunications Union
MIR	Ministère de l'Industrie et de la Recherche
NAB	National Association of Broadcasters
NASA	National Aeronautics and Space Administration
OC	Operating Committee of the Advisory Committee on Export Policy
OIRT	International Radio and Television Organization
ORTF	Organization de Radiodiffusion et Télévision Francaise
SMPTE	Society of Motion Picture and Television Engineers
UIR	International Broadcasting Union
UL	Underwriters' Laboratories
URSI	International Scientific Radio Union
URTNA	Union of National Radio and Television Organizations of Africa
UTE	Union Technique de l'Électricité
UAMPT	African and Malagasy Postal and Telecommunication Union
VDE	Verband Deutscher Elektrotechniker
WARC	World Administrative Radio Conference
WMO	World Meteorological Organization

B

Franco-Soviet Accord

ACCORD

Between the Government of the French Republic and the Government of the Union of the Soviet Socialist Republics on cooperation in the field of color television.

The Government of the French Republic and the Government of the Union of the Soviet Socialist Republics,

Consider that the multilateral development of peaceful cooperation between the countries of Europe will exercise a beneficial influence on the situation in Europe and on the entire world;

Estimate that the adoption of a single color television system by all European nations will have great influence on cooperation between European peoples and will favor the mutual knowledge of their lives and cultures. Underscore the considerable scientific and technological accomplishments in the field of color television in France and in the U.S.S.R., especially taking into consideration the positive results attained with the SECAM system;

Express their satisfaction at the establishment of direct liasons between the interested organizations in France and in the U.S.S.R. in this field, and value that the conclusion of an agreement of scientific and technological cooperation between The State Committee for the Coordination of Scientific and Technological Research in the U.S.S.R. and the companies C.S.F. and C.F.T. will constitute a substantial contribution to the execution of the accord;

Express the conviction that scientific and technological cooperation in the field of color television will contribute to the ulterior development of cooperation between the two countries in other fields of science and technology;

Firmly believe that cooperation in this field corresponds to the spirit of traditional friendliness between the French and Soviet peoples, are committed to the following:

Article 1 - The two governments will unite their effort in view of elaborating and putting into operation a common system of color television based on the SECAM standard. To this end, they will bring all their support in the organizations and companies concerned in the two countries in order to establish scientific, technological and economic cooperation between France and the U.S.S.R. in the field of color television.

Article 2 - This cooperation will be effectuated notably through communal scientific research, by studies, by establishing the organizations for series production and mutual sales of sets and technical equipment, by mutual sales and exchanges of licenses, by the organization stage by stage of experts, exchanges of information and scientific and technological documentation.

Article 3 - In order to ensure mutual consultation, the solution of concrete problems flowing from the present agreement, the definition of the methods and forms of scientific, technological and economic cooperation, the two parties institute, on a shared basis, a mixed Franco-Soviet commission composed of representatives to state organizations and industrial companies from the two countries.

Article 4 - The two parties sanction the adoption by all European countries of a single European color television system based on the SECAM standard. To this end, they will join their positions in international negotiations, conferences and congresses.

Article 5 - If necessary, the present accord can be made more precise, complete or modified by common consent between the two governments.

Article 6 - The present accord will take effect from the day it is signed and will be valid for a period of five years. If, one year preceeding its expiration date, neither party makes known a desire to break it, it will automatically be enforced for a new period of 5 years and similarly each subsequent renewal.

Bibliography

Accord entre le gouvernement de la République Francaise et le gouvernement de L'Union des Républiques Socialistes Soviétiques sur la cooperation dans le domaine de la télévision en couleurs. (1965). *Journal Officiel de la République Francaise* (July), 5763-5764.

Accord Franco-Egyptien pour l'expérimentation de SECAM. (1972). *Les Échos* (April 4).

Activities of the International Frequency Board. (1973). *Telecommunication Journal 40*, 402-406.

Ainsworth, C. (1964). Standardization abroad. *Magazine of Standards 35*, 364-367.

Air traffic control. (1965). *Electronics 38* (No. 24), 131-132.

Allen, A. (1966). International standardization and expanded world trade. *Magazine of Standards 37*, 191-194.

Anderson, E. V. (1976). The Tokyo round: How the U.S. chemical industry feels about it. *Chemical and Engineering News 54* (No. 5), 22-31.

Arabie Saudite. (1972). *Le Monde* (September 8), 1.

Arabie Saudite: M. Michel d'Ornaux est recu par le Roi Faycal. (1974). *Le Monde* (August 24).

Arnaud, J. (1970). SECAM: Le choix de l'Espagne dépend de facteurs qui dépassent la conjuncture actuelle. *Les Échos* (December 24).

Bachélard, R. (1972). "La Normalisation en France." (Unpublished manuscript).

Bachélard, R. (1974). "Étude Concernant la Normalisation dans les Neuf Pays Membres du Marché Commun." (Unpublished manuscript).

Baldwin, R. (1970). "Nontariff Distortions of International Trade." Brookings Institution, Washington, D.C.

La Bataille de la télé en boîte. (1971). *L'Auror* (April 8).

Des Batailles de prix qui ont coûté cher aux commercants. (1975). *Les Échos* (February 12).

Baum, W. (1958). "The French Economy and the State." Princeton University Press, Princeton, New Jersey.

Beadle, G. (1963). "Television—A Critical Review." Allen & Unwin, London.

Berrada, A. (1970). Some aspects of regulations for broadcasting. *Telecommunication Journal 37*, 639-646.

Bidwell, P. (1939). "The Invisible Tariff." Council on Foreign Relations, New York.

Birle, J. (1961). Standardization in France. *Magazine of Standards 32*, 106-109.

Bonn and U.S. reach accord on color TV. (1965). *New York Times* (April 7), p. 3.

Bourne, E. (1965). French TV blip blows conference. *Christian Science Monitor* (March 26).

Bruch, W. (1969). "Die Fernseh-Story." Franckh'sch Verlagshandlung, Stuttgart, Germany.

Business abroad: A rosy hue for color TV in Europe. (1966). *Business Week* (October 22), 94-98.

Business international: All PALS TOGETHER. (1966). *Economist 218*, 628-629.

Business international: Colour TV—Belgian cockpit. (1966). *Economist 220*, 288-290.

Business international: Colour TV: Each to his own. (1965). *Economist 214*, 1416.

Business international: Europe's mare nostrum. (1972). *Economist 244*, 66-67.

Business international: Italian television—awful choice. (1975). *Economist 254*, 91-92.

Business international: Italian television—colour politics. (1972). *Economist 244*, 74.

Business international: Italian television—too clever by half. (1972). *Economist* (August 19), 80.

Business international: Italy—PAL has enemies. (1971). *Economist 241*, 92, 96.

Business international: The politics of colour. (1965). *Economist 214*, 691-695.

Business international: You, too, can QAM. (1965). *Economist 215*, 215-216.

Calabuig, S. (1974). La "voix de la France" à l'étranger ne coûté guère plus qu'un "mirage." *Le Monde* (November 18), 16.

Carenzo, L. (1975). SECAM: La politique d'exportation en couleur. *Le Quotidien de Paris* (January 15), 1.

Castel, Y. (1967). La TV couleur en France: un démarrage lent. *Les Informations Industrielles et Commerciales* (September), 16-17.

Codding, G. (1952). "The International Telecommunications Union: An Experiment in International Cooperation." E. J. Brill, Leiden, Netherlands.

Codding, G. (1959). "Broadcasting Without Barriers." UNESCO, Paris.

Color TV choice in Italy draws fire of leftists. (1975). *International Herald Tribune* (April 12), p. 5.

Color TV ruling delayed by Italy. (1975). *International Herald Tribune* (April 4).

The colour situation: Three systems line up for battle at Vienna. (1965). *Wireless World 71* (No. 3), 130-131.

The coming battle for the color TV market. (1966). *Fortune 73*, 144-147, 188-195.

Comité Consultatif International des Télécommunications. (1967). "XIe Assemblée Plenière, Oslo, 1966; Analyse du Document: Doc 138," (July 1). Courtesy of M. Dubail, INTERSECAM, Paris, France.

Crane, R. J. (1977). International telecommunications standards—problems and progress. *Telephony* (May 16), 65-85.

Crane, R. J. (1978). Communication standards and the politics of protectionism. *Telecommunications Policy* (December), 267-281.

Curzon, G., & Curzon, V. (1970). "Hidden Barriers to International Trade." Trade Policy Research Centre, London.

Delacour, R. (1965). Controverse Franco-Allemand à propos de la télévision en couleurs. *Le Monde* (April 4-5), 15.

De Latil, P. (1967). Le Liban, troisième pays à émettre en SECAM. *Le Figaro* (November 9), 29.

De Latil, P. (1974a). La France se hâte lentement. *Le Figaro* (January 23).

De Latil, P. (1974b). Le marché de la télévision couleur a six ans. *Le Figaro* (January 16).

De Latil, P. (1974c). Le SECAM bien placé sur l'échiquier mondial. *Le Figaro* (February 8).

De Latil, P. (1974d). Les plus recents progrès de la télévision couleur. *Le Figaro* (April 8).

De Montalais, J. (1965). Un succès qui fait du bruit. *La Nation* (March 24).

Department of State Telegram to Amembassy in Moscow 2486, March 17, 1965. Edited and Declassified Document, October 21, 1975.

Department of State Telegram 1741 to Amembassy Moscow, December 22, 1964. Edited and Declassified Document, October 21, 1975.

Department of State Telegram to Amembassy Moscow 2222, February 17, 1965. Edited and Declassified Document, October 21, 1975.

Dibie, J.-N. (undated). "Exposé sur la promotion du procédé SECAM de télévision couleur." (Unpublished paper, courtesy of INTERSECAM, Paris, France.)

Dibie, J.-N. (1972). "Document de travail: Choix d'un procédé de télévision couleur par divers pays." Unpublished paper.

Dizard, W. R. (1966). "Television: A World View." Syrcause University Press, Syracuse, New York.

Durand, H., & Frontard, R. (1972). "Les Avantages Économiques de la Normalisation." Association Francaise de Normalisation, Paris.

Durieux, C. (1967). Les postes de TV-couleurs coûteront plus cher qu'a l'étranger en raison du double lignage. *Le Monde* (June 30), 1-4.

Durieux, C. (1974). Les émissions à destination de l'étranger vont-elles devoir limiter leurs objectifs? *Le Monde* (January 22).

Les Egyptiens se prononcent pour le procédé SECAM. (1969). *Le Monde* (January 22), 17.

Electronic Industries Association. (1965). "Color Television Systems: Summary of Differences Between NTSC, SECAM and PAL Color Television Systems." Electronic Industries Association, New York.

Electronic Industries Association. (1972). "The Electronic Industry in 1985: An Economic Forecast." Electronic Industries Assn., Washington, D.C.

Electronics abroad: Argentina. (1965). *Electronics.* (September).

Electronics abroad: Argentina—bridgehead for SECAM. (1965). *Electronics 38* (No. 17), 165.

Electronics abroad: Austria—color TV sweepstakes. (1965). *Electronics 38* (No. 2), 153-154.

Electronics abroad: France—African campaign. (1966). *Electronics 39* (No. 26), 169-170.

Electronics abroad: France—broken color line. (1968). *Electronics 41*, 236-237.

Electronics abroad: India—market for Red TV. (1965). *Electronics 38* (No. 23), 229-230.

Electronics abroad: Latin America—dumping PAL? (1968). *Electronics 41* (No. 17), 184-185.

Electronics abroad: Rumania. (1965). *Electronics 38* (No. 4), 189.

Electronics international: Sweden—dimming the color. (1969). *Electronics 42* (No. 17), 198.

Emery, W. B. (1966). "Five European Broadcasting Systems." *Journalism Monograms 1.*

Erikson, A. (1966). Consumer electronics: Europe split on color TV. *Electronics 39* (No. 12), 161-165.

Escarpit, R. (1965). L'arc-en-ciel. *Le Monde* (March 24), 1.

European Broadcasting Union. (1966). "Report of the E.B.U. Ad-Hoc Group on Colour Television." European Broadcasting Union Technical Centre, Brussels, Belgium.

European components standards accord labeled a threat to trade by U.S. (1970). *Electronics E* (May 30), 39.

Ewert, I. (1969). The U.S. role in world standardization. *Magazine of Standards 40*, 48-51.

Fauques, N. (1965). Toutes que vous devez savoir sur la T.V.-couleur Francaise. *La Nation* (March 24).

Fédération Nationale des Industries Électroniques. (1974). "Annuaire Edition 1974." Fédération Nationale des Industries Électroniques, Paris.

Fight goes worldwide for color TV sales (1964). *Business Week* (May 30), 44-48.

Fijalkowski, W. J. (1965). The I.T.U. *Telecommunication Journal 32*, 205-212.

Franklin, R. H. (1966). Compatability in world communications. *IEEE Spectrum 3* (No. 10), 73-77.

French TV makers hope tax cut will end sales slump . . . while British market flourishes. (1970). *Electronics 43* (No. 18), 133.

Friesth, E. F. (1970). The United States role in world standardization. *Magazine of Standards 41*, 93-96.

From Russia with love—a political compromise colour television system? (1966). *Wireless World 72*, 73.

Froste, F. C. (1962). What is ASA? Principles and concepts of the American Standards Association. *Magazine of Standards 33*, 214-216.

Gadonneix, P. (1974). "The Influence of the State on Industrial Strategies: A Study of the Computer Industry in France." (Unpublished dissertation, Harvard Business School.)

Galuce, R. (1965). Echèc aux Américains? *Le Capital* (March 30).

Le Générale de Gaulle "la sympathie séculaire et l'affinite naturelle portent les Francais et les Russes à se rapprocher en dépit de tous les obstacles." (1965). *Le Monde* (March 24).

Geren, P. F. (1965). Worldwide standards for color television. *U.S. State Department Bulletin 53*, 597-601.

Gilpin, R. (1968). "France in the Age of the Scientific State." Princeton University Press, Princeton, New Jersey.

Gilpin, R. (1970). Technological strategies and national purpose. *Science 169*, 441-448.

Goar Mestre, deploring "standstill," to lead Argentina into age of color TV. (1969). *Variety* (September 10), 102.

Gould, J. (1966). TV: Soviet Union offers color system. *New York Times* (March 16).

Gould, R. (1971). International telecommunications organizations and how they affect you. *Electronics World 85* (No. 2), 38-41.

Le gouvernement Grèc dénonce un accord d'équipement de télévision en couleurs conclu avec Page-Europa. (1969). *Le Monde* (January 17).

Graubard, S., ed. (1963). "A New Europe." Beacon Press, Boston, Massachusetts.

Green T. (1972). "The Universal Eye." The Bodley Head, London.

Grove, A. (1966). International standardization—interface with the future. *I.E.E.E. Spectrum 3* (No. 8), 91-101.

Guéry, C. (1975). Industrie de la TV couleur: pas de crise, mais . . . *Le Figaro* (November 21).

Halberstrom, D. (1966). France and Soviet Union deny troubles in joint color-TV plan. *New York Times* (January 29, pp. 31, 37.

Hansen, G. (1964). Colour television standards for Europe? *In* "World Radio TV Handbook," Vol. 18 (O. L. Johansen, ed.), O. L. Johansen, Hellerup, Denmark, 40-41.

Hansen, G. (1966). Colour television in Europe. *European Broadcasting Union Review—Part A—Technical* (No. 98), (August), pp. 138-141.

Harlow, J. (1966). "French Economic Planning." Iowa University Press, Iowa City, Iowa.

Hemmendinger, N. (1964). "Non-Tariff Trade Barriers of the United States." United States-Japan Trade Council, Washington, D.C.

Herbstreit, J., & Poliquen, H. (1967). International standards for colour television. *Telecommunication Journal 34*, 16-23.

Herbstreit, J., & Pouliquen, H. (1967). International standards for colour television. *IEEE Spectrum* (March), 104-111.

Hirsch, C. (1967). Introduction to a panel discussion of color television systems. *IEEE Spectrum* (March), pp. 147-149.

Hirsch, C. (1968). Color television standards for region 2. *IEEE Spectrum* (February), 62-67.

Hoffman, S. D. (1962). What is ASA? The sectional committee method. *Magazine of Standards* (September), 276-278.

Hoffman, S. D. (1963). Standards, antitrust and the Common Market. *Magazine of Standards* (February), 46-47.

Hoffman, S. D. (1963). The IEC in France. *Magazine of Standards* (June), 186-187.

Hoffman, S. D. (1963). The U.S. National Committee of the IEC. *Magazine of Standards 34* (No. 6), 186-187.

Hoffman, S. D. (1964). The IEC in France. *Magazine of Standards* (June).

Hoffmann, S. (ed) (1963). "In Search of France." Harper & Row, New York.

Holland, J. N. (1968). New directions on cable standardization. *Electronics World 80* (No. 4), 37.

Holland, S. (1974). Europe's new public enterprises. *In* "Big Business and the State" (R. Vernon, ed.), pp. 25-44. Harvard University Press, Cambridge, Massachusetts.

La Hongrie adopte le procédé Francais de télévision en couleurs. (1969). *Le Monde* (January 24).

Houser, R. C., & Frahm, S. (1974). Technology, trade and the law. *Law and Policy in International Business 6* (No. 85), 85-149.

How CEN works to coordinate national standards. (1963). *Magazine of Standards 34* (No. 10), 309-310.

How we use ASA procedures. (1964). *Magazine of Standards 35*, 103-104.

Humphrey, R. (1968). Geneva conference affects marine communications. *Electronics World 79* (No. 2), 42.

Il faut unifier les standards de notre télévision. (1967). *France-Soir* (June 28).

L'industrie électronique Francaise s'occupe une place très honorable sur le plan international. (1966). *L'Information* (April 21), 1.

Industry asks federal export aid. (1972). *Electronics 45* (No. 15), 53-54.

International newsletter: What color TV system will Italy choose? (1972). *Electronics 45* (No. 18), 47.

International report: Spain—trouble with the neighbours. (1975). *Economist 255*, 33.

International Standards Organization. (1971). "Études sur les Marques de Conformité aux Normes." International Standards Organization, Geneva, Switzerland.

Introducing the U.S.A. Standards Institute. (1966). *Magazine of Standards 37*, 287-289.

Italian experts ask selection of German color TV system. (1975). *International Herald Tribune* (April 4), 1.

Italie: Les republicans menacent de quitter la majorité si le système de télévision SECAM est adopté. (1972). *Le Monde* (August 18).

Italie: Rendez-vous en Sardaigne par MM. Jobert et Medici. (1973). *Le Monde* (May 26).

Italie: Rome dément avoir subi des pressions de Paris en faveur du procédé SECAM. (1972). *Le Monde* (August 28), 5.

Jones, W. J. (1973). The role of international standardization in telecommunication development. *Telecommunication Journal 40*, 207-210.

Jublin, J. (1974). EMO (Group Floriat) passe dans le groin de téléfunken: la télévision couleur marque le pas dans les pays Européens. *Les Échos* (October 29).

Jublin, J. (1975). Le SECAM adopté par 20 pays rapportera plusieurs milliards. *Les Échos* (February 12).

Kelley, W. B., Jr. (1967). Nontariff barriers. *In* "Studies in Trade Liberalization" (B. Balassa, ed.), pp. 265-314. John Hopkins University Press, Baltimore, Maryland.

Kilborn, P. (1966). Electronics for grandeur: De Gaulle's foreign policy spurs growth of CSF. *Electronics 39*, 224-228.

Lachenbruch, D. (1966). Color TV around the world. *Electronic Age* (Autumn), 3-5.

Lamb, H. C. (1962). What is ASA? A short history of the American Standards Association. *Magazine of Standards 33*, 180-181.

Landes, D. (1969). "The Unbound Prometheus: Technological Change and Industrial Development in Western Europe from 1970 to the Present." Cambridge University Press, London.

La Que, F. (1969). ISO—a global view. *Magazine of Standards 40*, 144-146.

Lavallard, J.-L. (1965). L'accord Franco-Soviétique sur la télévision en couleurs. *Le Monde* (March 24), 2-3.

Lavallard, J.-L. (1973). Quand la télévision en noir et blanc aura disparu. *Le Monde* (July 25), 2.

Lavéron, M. (1975). L'industrie électronique Francaise en 1975. *Industries Électriques et Électroniques* (No. 12).

Layton, C. (1972). "Ten Innovations." Allen & Unwin, London.

Letter from Radio Corporation of America to Office of Export Control, December 17, 1964. Edited and Declassified Document, October 21, 1975.

Letter from Radio Corporation of America to Office of Export Control, December 18, 1964. Edited and Declassified Document, October 21, 1975.

Le Liban se prononce en faveur du procédé Francais. (1969). *Le Monde* (February 11).

La Libye s'intéresse au système SECAM de télévision couleur. (1971). *Le Monde* (July 30).

Lilt, A. (1967). L'avenir n'est pas rosé pour la TV couleurs. *Communauté Européene* (No. 111) (October), 14-15.

May, J. A. (1965). France bests U.S. on color TV. *Christian Science Monitor* (March 27).

McElheny, V. K. (1966). Franco-Russian collaboration in science: De Gaulle's visit. *Science 153*, 43-46.

McLean, F. (1966). Worldwide color television standards. *IEEE Spectrum 3* (No. 6), 59. (Also published in *IEEE Transactions: Broadcast and Television Receivers BTR-12* (No. 2), 42.)

McQuade, L. (1971). U.S. trade with Eastern Europe: Its prospects and parameters. *Law and Policy in International Business 3* (No. 42), 41-100.

Mallein, S. (1965a). Quid du Quam? *Radio et TV* (June), 15-16.

Mallein, S. (1965b). Bonnes images de Russie. *Radio et TV* (December), 17-18.

Malmgren, H. B. (1970). "Trade Wars or Trade Negotiations? Nontariff Barriers and Economic Peacekeeping." Atlantic Council of the United States, Washington, D.C.

Massel, M. K. (1965). Non-Tariff barriers as an obstacle to world trade. *In* "The Expansion of World Trade: Legal Problems and Techniques" (D. Thompson, ed.), pp. 61-72. British Institute of International and Comparative Law, London. (Brookings Report 97.)

Meeting fails to set color TV standards. (1965). *Broadcasting 68* (April 12), 64-65.

"Memorandum of Conference." (1965). "Subject: RCA Color Television System for Soviet Bloc." (Edited and Declassified Document, October 21, 1975). Dept. of Commerce, Washington, D.C.

"Memorandum of November 17, 1964." (Edited and Declassified Document, October 21, 1975.) (I-29409/64) from Defense OC member to Chairman, OC. Operating Committee, Advisory Committee on Export Policy, Dept. of Commerce, Washington, D.C.

"Memorandum of November 30, 1964." (I-29776/64) from Defense OC Member to Chairman, OC. Edited and Declassified Document, October 21, 1975.

"Memorandum to Secretary Hodges." "Subject: Recommendation of RCA Color Television Tape Recorder in Moscow, USSR, December 22, 1964." Edited and Declassified Document, October 21, 1975.

"Memorandum to Mr. Wyman, March 22, 1965." Edited and Declassified Document, October 21, 1975.

"Memorandum to Secretary Connor." "Subject: Background Paper on Proposed Export of RCA Color TV System to Soviet Bloc for ECRB Meeting, March 11, 1965." Edited and Declassified Document, October 21, 1975.

"Memorandum Entitled Differences between NTSC (RCA) and SECAM Color TV Systems. Undated." Edited and Declassified Document, October 21, 1975.

"Memorandum to the Secretary." "Subject: Briefing Paper for ECRB Meeting on Proposed Export of RAC Color TV System to East European Communist Countries. Undated." Edited and Declassified Document, October 21, 1975.

Metzger, S. (1974). "Lowering Nontariff Barriers." Brookings Institution, Washington, D.C.

Mexicans learn to read and write on color television. (1965). *Washington Post* (December 25).

Michalet, C. (1974). France. *In* "Big Business and the State" (R. Vernon, ed.), pp. 105-126. Harvard University Press, Cambridge, Massachusetts.

Mikton, R. (1963). Europe's color TV competition. *Electronics 36* (No. 31), 22-23.

Mili, M. (1973a). International jurisdiction in telecommunications affairs—the recommendations II. *Telecommunication Journal 40,* 746-749.

Mili, M. (1973b). International jurisdiction in telecommunication affairs—the regulations—I. *Telecommunication Journal 40,* 286-290.

Mili, M. (1973c). International jurisdiction in telecommunication affairs—the regulations—II. *Telecommunication Journal 40,* 344-348.

Mili, M. (1973d). International jurisdiction in telecommunication affairs. *Telecommunication Journal 40,* 122-128.

Mili, M. (1973e). International jurisdiction in telecommunication matters—the connection. *Telecommunication Journal 40,* 174-182.

Mili, M. (1974). International jurisdiction in telecommunication affairs—conclusion. *Telecommunication Journal 41* (No. 3J, 170-172.

M. Jobert en Espagne. (1973). *Le Monde* (August 28), 1.

Mooney, R. E. (1965). Soviet endorses French color T.V. *New York Times* (March 23), Sect. 1, p. 1.

Mooney, R. E. (1965). French pushing their color T.V. system. *New York Times* (May 9), Section 3, p. 14.

Move to promote U.S. color abroad starts. (1964). *Broadcasting 67* (No. 14), 76.

Naumurois, A. (1972). "European Broadcasting Union—Structures and Organization of Broadcasting in the Framework of Radiocommunications." European Broadcasting Union, Geneva, Switzerland.

Nelson, R. (1968). "The Technology Gap: Analysis and Appraisal." (Paper presented at a conference sponsored by the Agnelli Foundation and the Tocqueville Project of the Twentieth Century Fund held in Turin, Italy, November 17-19.)

Nelson, R. (1971). "World leadership," the "technological gap" and national policy. *Minerva 9,* 386-399.

New British device facilitates U.S. color-TV link to Europe. (1967). *New York Times* (March 14), p. 95.

New nations show muscle in I.T.U. (1965). *Broadcasting 69* (December 6), 71-72.

Newsletter from abroad: Color-set prices shaved in France. (1968). *Electronics 41* (No. 10), 191.

Newsletter from abroad: Spain jockeying to make the most of color TV split. (1966). *Electronics 39* (No. 20), 251.

Newsletter from abroad: Telefunken devices may mend color TV split in Europe. (1967). *Electronics 40* (No. 10), 227-228.

Nicotera, F. (1964). The structure of the ITU. *Telecommunication Journal 31,* 157-165.

Nyehan, E. M. (1967). "Color Television—Lebanon." (Unpublished paper.) Electronics Division, Business and Defense Services Administration, U.S. Dept. of Commerce, Washington, D.C.

Nyehan, E. M. (1968). A Common Television System for the Americas. (Unpublished paper.) (Revised.) Electronics Division, Business and Defense Services Administration, U.S. Dept. of Commerce, Washington, D.C.

Oganesoff, I. (1965). France and U.S. Battle over color TV system for Europe; RCA has big stake. *Wall Street Journal* (March 3), 10.

Olmer, P. (1968). TV coleur: des prix plus abordables. *La Vie Francaise* (April 5).

Paris et Rome envisagent des initiatives conjointes en Mediterranée. (1970). *Le Monde* (May 22), 1, 4.

Parker, N. (1967). The cost of using PAL, or SECAM and possible improvements in NTSC receivers. *IEEE Spectrum* (March), pp. 159-161.

Parrott, M. (1966). The politics of colour television. *World Today* 22, 252-260.

Passeron, A. (1974a). Iran: les vastes projets de cooperation économique sont au centre des entretiens de M. Chirac à Téhéran. *Le Monde* (December 21), 1.

Passeron, A. (1974b). La volonté de coopération Franco-Iranienne se manifeste par l'adoption du procédé SECAM et le lancement d'importants projets industriels. *Le Monde* (December 24), 1.

Passeron, A. (1974c). Le voyage du Premier Ministre à Téhéran: La France deviendra le premier fournisseur de l'Iran. *Le Monde* (December 21), 1.

Patterson, G. (1966). "Discrimination in International Trade, the Policy Issues 1945-65." Princeton University Press, Princeton, New Jersey.

Paulu, B. (1970). "Broadcasting on the European Continent." University of Minnesota Press, Minneapolis, Minnesota.

Peyrefitte a entretenu les ministres Espagnols les problèmes de la télévision en couleurs. (1966). *Le Monde* (October 18), 3.

Philips fabriquera les trois systèmes de TV couleurs. (1967). *France-Soir* (July 11).

Picapier, J.-P. (1969). En Allemagne de l'Est—inauguration des émissions en couleurs avec le procédé SECAM. *Le Monde* (October 10).

Podolsky, L. (1968). The name of the game, or how to play standards for foreign markets. *Magazine of Standards 39*, 44-45.

Polaroid sues Kodak. (1976). *Time* (May 10), 64.

Political hues. (1966). *Wireless World 72*, 431.

Pouliquen, H. (1966). The International Radio Consultative Committee. *Telecommunication Journal 33*, 224-234.

Price, L. (1966a). European standards affecting the appliance industry. *Magazine of Standards 37*, 205-209.

Price, L. (1966b). NEMA's role in standardization. *Magazine of Standards 37*, 232-237.

Proche-Orient: la visite du Roi Faycal à Paris s'achève. (1973). *Le Monde* (May 18), 6.

Pulling, M. (1963). "International Television." British Broadcasting Company, London. (BBC Lunchtime Lecture Series, January 9, 1963.)

R.C.A. in Russia selling color TV. (1964). *Business Week* (May 30)

Recent work of the C.C.I.R. Study Group on television. (1950, 1951). *European Broadcasting Union Bulletin 1* (No. 2), 132-142; 2 (No. 5), 28-37.

Remley, F. (1966). C.C.I.R.-Oslo, 1966: A report on international radio and television standardization. *SMPTE Journal* (October), 42-47.

Rennick, J. L. (1967). "A brief description of SECAM III A. *IEEE Spectrum* (March), 150-152.

Restrictive effects of industrial standards on international commerce. (1972). *Law and Policy in International Business 4*, 607-627.

Robertson, J. (1976). Government closeup: MLS—a Grimm Tale. *Electronic News* (February 19).

Rockwell, W. (1970). International trade: The impact of certification. *Magazine of Standards 41*, 77-79.

Roman, A. V. (1967). "The Historical Development of Color Television Systems." Unpublished dissertation, New York University.

Ruppert, L., and Stanford, C. J. (1967). Impact of the IEC's work on world trade. *Magazine of Standards 36*, 262-264.

Russia backs French color TV system, but R.C.A. is still in profits race in Europe. (1965). *Business Week* (March 27), p. 36.

Russia joins France in favoring SECAM for Europe's color TV over RCA system. (1965). *Wall Street Journal* (March 23), p. 3.

Salomon, J. -J. (1971). Europe and the technology gap. *International Studies Quarterly 15*, 5-31.

Scherer, F. (1970). "Industrial Market Structure and Economic Performance." Rand McNally, New York.

Schindler, M. (1964). L'affaire Bull: symptôme de la crise d'aptatation de l'économie Européene. *La Gazette de Lausanne* (May 21), 1.

Schwoebel, J. (1973). La coopération Franco-Yugoslave dans les pays tiers sera renforcée. *Le Monde* (May 31).

Le Secam en Afrique. (1971). *Le Monde* (September 13).

"Selection of a World-Wide N.T.S.C. Colour Television System." (1966). Subject, Question 118/XI. Document XI/170-E. June 28, 1966. C.C.I.R. Study Group Period 1963-1966.

Servan-Schreiber, J. J. (1967). "Le défi Américain." Denoël, Paris.

Shonfield, A. (1965). "Modern Capitalism." University Press, Oxford, England.

Should foreign parts be labelled? (1966). *Broadcasting 70* (No. 2), 70-71.

Silverstein, L. L., and Reale, U., eds. (1973). "The Enlarged European Community: Legal Challenges for American Business." Practicing Law Institute, New York.

Skolnikoff, E. B. (1967). "Science, Technology and American Foreign Policy." M.I.T. Press, Cambridge, Massachusetts.

Skolnikoff, E. B. (1972). "The International Imperatives of Technology: Technological Development and the International System." Institute of International Studies, University of California, Berkeley, Berkeley, California (Research Series 190.16.)

Smith, D. (1969). "International Telecommunications Control." W. W. Sijthoff, Leyden, Netherlands.

Sole, R. (1975a). L'Italie pourrait adopter son propre procédé pour les émissions en couleurs. *Le Monde* (February 25).

Sole, R. (1975b). L'Italie pourrait lever à la fin de Mars les mésures de restriction aux importations. *Le Monde* (February 16).

Soviet endorses French color TV. (1965). *New York Times* (March 23) p. 1.

Spencer, L. (1970). "Technology Gap in Perspective: Strategy of International Technology Transfer." Spartan Books, New York.

Standardization and the development of trade. (1964). *Magazine of Standards 35*, 237.

Standards: Barriers or aids to commerce and trade? (1970). *Magazine of Standards 41*, 10-11.

Struglia, E. (1965). "Standards, Specifications, and Information Sources." Gale Research Company, Detroit, Michigan.

Tandis que l'Iran adopte le procédé SECAM: les entretiens de M. Chirac à Téhéran ont permis d'accélérer la conclusion d'importants contrats. (1974). Le Monde (December 24), pp. 22-23.

Tatu, M. (1974a). Les contrats signés ou prévus entre la France et l'Irak porteront sur un montrant global de 15 milliards. Le Monde (December 4).

Tatu, M. (1974b). M. Chirac à Bagdad et à Athènes. Le Monde (December 3), 1, 2, 37.

Taxe spéciale pour la TV-couleur en 1974? (1973). Le Monde (July 4).

Tchécoslovaquie—Paris et Prague concluront une convention de coopération pour la télévision en couleurs. (1967). Le Monde (November 21).

Technical cooperation and the International Radio Consultative Committee. (1973). Telecommunication Journal 40, 408-414.

Technology: A bitter dispute over landing systems. (1975). Business Week (March 3), 58-60.

La télévision en couleurs en Italie: INTERSECAM affirme n'avoir pas tenté de corrompre des personnalités. (1972). Le Monde (August 20), 1.

Temple, C. (1968). INTERSECAM fera valoir les couleurs Francaises. France-Soir (March 14)., 1.

Tessier, J. (1975). "SOFRATEV." Unpublished memo. Courtesy of Société Francaise d'Études et de Réalisations d'Équipements de Radio-diffusion et de la Télévision, Paris, France (April 10).

Theile, R. (1963). The work of the Ad Hoc Group on colour television. European Broadcasting Union Review—Part A—Technical (No. 80A), (August).

Theile, R. (1965). The development of compatible colour television with par-ticular reference to the different proposals for transmitting the chrominance signals. European Broadcasting Union Review—Part A—Technical (No. 93), (October).

Thélier, A. (1969). La télévision en couleurs Italienne-a-t-elle renoncé définitive-ment au procédé Francais? Le Monde (June 10), 1, 2, 3.;

TV conference splits over color systems: Votes favor French. (1965). Wall Street Journal (April 8), p. 10.

TV: La couleur et le noir et blanc coéxisteront pacifiquement—du fait du coût élévé des recepteurs couleur. (1966). Combat (December 18), 1.

United Nations. (1968). "Everyman's United Nations." United Nations, New York.

United Nations. (1971, 1972, 1975). "World Trade Annual," Walker and Com-pany, New York.

L'U.R.S.S. choisit le procédé Francais de télévision en couleurs. (1965). Le Monde (March 23), 1.

U.S. Dept. of Commerce. (1964). "OC Document 2606 (November 4, 1964)," (Edited and Declassified Document, October 21, 1975. Subject: Reexport of color television tape recorder to USSR for demonstra-tion and sale; attachments and OC minutes.) Operating Committee, Advisory Committee on Export Policy, Dept. of Commerce, Washington, D.C.

U.S. Export Control Review Board. (1965). "Summary of Minutes of Export Control Review Board Meeting of March 12, 1965." (Edited and Declassified Document, October 21, 1975.) Export Control Review Board, Dept. of Commerce, Washington, D.C.

U.S. and Bonn agree to merge color TV systems. (1965). *New York Times* (April 7), 3.

USASI's foreign service to industry. (1968). *Magazine of Standards 39,* 24-25.

U.S., Bonn color TV is Europe's second. (1965). *New York Tribune* (April 7).

U.S. participation in IEC: Review and evaluation. (1966). *Magazine of Standards 37,* 238-241.

U.S. TV hops to Europe via digital converter. (1972). *Electronics 45* (No. 23), 58.

U.S., West Germany adopt compromise plan for color T.V. system. (1965). *Wall Street Journal* (April 7), p. 7.

Valensi, G. (1965). The development of international telephony. *Telecommunication Journal 32,* 9-17.

Varis, T. (1973). "International Inventory of Television Programme Structure and the Flow of TV Programmes Between Nations." Research Institute and Institute of Journalism and Mass Communication, University of Tampere, Tampere, Finland.

Vernon, R., ed. (1974). "Big Business and the State." Harvard University Press, Cambridge, Massachusetts.

Vichney, N. (1965a). La conférence sur la télévision en couleurs s'ouvre à Vienne dans un climat tendu. *Le Monde* (March 25).

Vichney, N. (1965b). Pourra-t-on empêcher la carte Européene de la télévision en couleurs d'être une mosaique? *Le Monde* (March 29).

Vichney, N. (1965c). Le procédé Francais de télévision en couleurs emporte la majorité des suffrages dans un vote consultatif. *Le Monde* (April 3), 11.

Vichney, N. (1965d). Télévision en couleurs: En dépit d'un rapprochement de dernière minute entre les procédés Américains et Allemands. *Le Monde* (April 8), 6.

Vichney, N. (1968). L'Argentine adopterait le procédé Francais de télévision en couleurs. *Le Monde* (March 12).

Vichney, N. (1974). Les nouvelles cathédrales pp. 1, 11: La foi—I; Les bâtisseurs—p. 11, II; Les démolisseurs—p. 12, III. *Le Monde* (November 5, 6, 7).

Vienna color T.V. parley is a failure. (1965). *New York Times* (April 8), p. 5.

La visite du Chah d'Iran? (1974). *Le Monde* (June 28), 3.

Wallenstein, G. (1972). International telecommunications where cooperation is the message. *Telecommunication Journal 39,* 365-370.

Wallenstein, G. (1974). The internationalization of telecommunications systems development. *Telecommunication Journal 41,* 33-38.

Warnke, P. C., and Morris, J. P. (1969). National security and international business. *Law and Policy in International Business 1* (No. 77), 77-105.

Weller, L. (1966). Compatibility a worldwide problem. *Electronics* (June 27).

Westfall, T. B. (1966). Global cables and satellite communication. *IEEE Spectrum 3* (No. 10), 64-66.

Wetz, J. (1972). Allemagne Fédérale: à son retour de Pékin M. Scheel confirme l'intérêt de la Chine pour une Europe Occidentale forte. *Le Monde* (November 5).

Will Europe face the American challenge? (1972). *Business Week* (October 14), 60-68.

Wingert, L. (1966). Progress in worldwide telephone dialing. *IEEE Spectrum 3* (No. 10), 67-69.

Woodward, C. (1972). "BSI the Story of Standards." British Standards Institution, London.

Zakharov, I. P., Denisenko, I. N., and Pevznei, B. M. (1964). "Selection of a Color Television System—USSR." U.S. Department of Commerce Clearinghouse for Federal Scientific and Technical Information, Washington, D.C. (Document JPRS; 26, 944;TT:64-51101.)

Zinzen, A. (1963). DIN standards—the work of the German Standards Association. *Magazine of Standards 34,* 363-367.

Zysman, J. (1974). "French Industry between the Market and the State." Unpublished dissertation, Massachusetts Institute of Technology.

Author Index

Page numbers in *italics* indicate where complete references are listed.

Subject Index